working with
psychic
protection

working with
psychic
protection

how to create positive, protective and healing energies

Teresa Moorey

A GODSFIELD BOOK
www.godsfield.co.uk

An Hachette Livre UK Company

First published in Great Britain in 2007 by
Godsfield Press, a division of Octopus Publishing Group Ltd
2–4 Heron Quays, London E14 4JP

Distributed in the United States and Canada by
Sterling Publishing Co., Inc.
387 Park Avenue South, New York, NY 10016–8810

ISBN-13: 978-184181-322-6
ISBN-10: 1-84181-322-2

A CIP catalogue record of this book is available from the
British Library.

Printed and bound in China

10 9 8 7 6 5 4 3 2 1

contents

INTRODUCTION

We are all well aware that life today is stressful. There are pressures on us from all sides and many people feel under bombardment, longing for an oasis of peace and safety. Sometimes we have a general feeling of being vulnerable and 'out of synch'. We may sense a 'bad atmosphere' around us, or be aware of something more specific, such as an actual attack of some kind, by a person or group of people. While imagination and negative thinking are part of the picture, they are certainly not the whole explanation for these feelings.

You may be reassured to know that there are effective and time-honoured ways of dealing with subtle threats. It is a question of learning some basic facts and putting into practice some simple routines that can make a radical difference to our feelings of security and wellbeing.

Phobias, panic attacks, anxiety and insomnia are just a few of the manifestations of the need for psychic 'hygiene' and psychic protection. Of course, these anxieties can be dealt with by other means, such as medication, but this does not get to the root cause of our uneasiness, and may be part of the picture of vulnerability and powerlessness that makes us feel unsafe and out of control in life.

The following pages take you through a practical, focused course that aims to help you clarify your awareness, strengthen yourself and inwardly cleanse yourself and your environment. It also teaches you to take steps towards solid protection from emotional and spiritual forces that seek, whether intentionally or unintentionally, to deplete and harm you.

The best discovery awaiting you is that in developing your inner strength you open yourself to the peace and beauty that is and always has been around all of us!

Teresa Moorey

*Serenity can open you to the peace
and beauty that surround you.*

learning strength and awareness

During my early teens I became aware that I was not like most other people – I was far more sensitive. Being with some people disturbed me quite deeply, to the point where I felt I was losing my identity. After such encounters, I needed to be alone for an hour or so in order to regain a sense of balance.

psychic vulnerability

Many things upset me profoundly. Seeing a tree being brutally chopped down rendered me almost hysterical because I could sense its suffering and its mute desperation to remain alive. Sometimes I wanted to curl up into a little ball to escape from all the unhappiness in the world, to which I seemed connected by invisible antennae. Like many children, I was sometimes rejected by my peers, and while putting on a brave face in public, inwardly I was devastated. Certain places also affected me with chills and premonitions. Had I not possessed a lively interest in the spirit world I might have decided I was simply neurotic. Instead, I realized that I was 'picking up' subtle messages and gradually I learned to protect myself from this vulnerability.

awareness of other realities

Of course, the dividing line between neurosis and psychic sensitivity is a thin one. In the following pages you will be encouraged to get to know yourself and to be very honest with yourself. In a loving and accepting fashion you can become aware how far and in what way you may be making yourself vulnerable – we all need 'protection' from our own inner demons and a little self-awareness!

Psychic protection is about being safe from anything unseen: from the strain of aggressive and selfish people, through the subtle effects of places and 'atmospheres', to more intentional attacks of a spiritual nature. It is important to realize that there are other dimensions to existence apart from the physical, day-to-day stuff we call 'reality', and to understand that the world provides us with plenty of energy-sources to help us defend ourselves.

enhance your personal power

The first and most important step to psychic protection is to strengthen oneself. We will look at a variety of ways to build health of mind and body and enhance personal power. Secondly, in order to defend your 'castle' it needs to be clean from within — you will learn beautiful and heartening ways to clear yourself and your home of any undermining negativity.

The actual business of protection and the ways towards safety are paths of balance and beauty. There are many simple, practical and effective things you can do to ensure you and your loved ones are protected in all areas of life — and the bonus is that these observances heighten your awareness, making life more enjoyable.

If you feel that you need protection, do not think of this as a sign of weakness but of awareness. As you become more used to protecting yourself you will see that this awareness is a special gift, enabling you to see the wonders in life and to spread joy around you.

Turn your face to the sun and relax, knowing you are in harmony with creation and held safely by the living Cosmos.

Strength, balance and a sense of beauty are all part of the path to protection.

WHAT IS PSYCHIC PROTECTION?

Psychic protection is really about protection of all kinds, starting with mental attitude, which is the most fundamental. This means being safe from the negative thoughts of others, from the depressing effects of certain places and also from real malevolence that may be directed against you. However, psychic protection deals with these issues in a non-combative way, concentrating on inner peace and balance and a positive attitude. If we respond to these negative influences with aggression and anger, these may feed the very negativity we are seeking to repel, even encouraging its growth within ourselves. By contrast, tranquillity and spiritual wholesomeness can make us invulnerable and full of happiness into the bargain!

True psychic protection also offers some physical protection, since much is conveyed by body language. Among animals, attack is often played out by ritual movements rather than by inflicting harm – the vanquished animal can slink away unharmed having indicated surrender, while the victor holds his position simply because of 'attitude'. Likewise, humans convey a myriad of messages by the way we move and hold ourselves. While it would be a mistake to rely on body language in the proverbial 'dark alley', it is nonetheless a powerful element in self-defence.

To make the best use of this chapter, allow yourself to be open to the idea of subtle energies that involve and affect us all, and be willing to experience and learn about these. We shall be looking at a variety of challenging situations in which you may need protection, and also at the energy-sources you can tap into in order to be in harmony with your surroundings and feel truly secure.

dealing with groups

A sense of inner poise and power can help in dealing with groups both at work and socially.

Many of us find situations involving large groups of people intimidating, especially if we are going to be playing a key role, such as chairing a meeting. This reaction is not unreasonable, for not so very long ago to be rejected by the tribe to which we belonged could be dangerous.

group dynamics

The eminent analytical psychologist Carl Jung (1875–1961) observed that in groups it is usually the lowest common denominator that dominates. The most powerful shared feelings of the group rise to the surface and carry much more weight than individual emotions. This sort of situation affects people in different ways. Fear communicates itself and some people respond with aggression, others with panic, although this takes place on a subconscious level. Others find themselves acting as spokesperson or behaving in surprising ways, finding themselves 'acting out' what others repress. In such circumstances I have often found myself being 'taken over' by something that is not the usual 'me'. In some situations, such as at a pop concert, this can be fun, while in other circumstances it is less pleasant. It is important to be able to step back, detach, become centred within yourself and place around yourself a protective psychic bubble, as explained in *Protection techniques*.

Group dynamics are usually present within the day-to-day working environment and in social situations. Office politics may bring out the worst in people and civilized individuals may behave in ways that are surprising! Adopt an attitude of benign detachment and as much humour as you can muster in these circumstances!

lower spirit entities

Occultists are aware of entities that feed off the energy in a crowd – lower spirit entities called 'elementals' thrive on disturbance. (These are not to be confused with the Elemental representatives of the four elements, Air, Fire, Earth and Water.) At some level you may be aware of these entities and feel threatened, so it is important to protect yourself.

archetypes

However, the group itself is an 'entity', shaped by the collective mind of the people involved. The collective unconscious (a term coined by Jung) is inhabited by 'archetypes' or universal forces. The ancients recognized these powers and worshipped them as gods. In *Protection techniques* you can find out about honouring these gods, enlisting their help and giving them due place. The gods that move within a crowd may be scary – Eris, the Greek goddess of discord, for instance, or warlike Mars.

It is true that these archetypes/gods are a necessary part of existence, and we all have to accept such things as anger, confusion and change in our lives. Nonetheless, there is a difference between working with such forces on our own terms and being on the receiving end of them through the actions of others.

While it is important to acknowledge the links you have with the group and the feelings that may be aroused in you, you can choose what to do with these feelings. Similarly, you can protect yourself from anything negative sent your way by your group and you can call on beings far stronger than the group mind to assist you (see *Protection techniques*, *Drawing positive energies* and *Advanced matters*).

in the home

Home is a place where we feel safe; we can be ourselves and can regroup after confrontations with a difficult world. Ironically, we are at our most vulnerable at home, because here we are open. To be truly psychically protected, you need a home-space that is peaceful, supportive and accepting. This is a vital first step on the way to building your security that you be honest with yourself about your home circumstances.

not like the movies

Flowers add to the positive aura of your home, although they may be too energizing for the bedroom.

Family life is rarely like a happy Disney film and flatmates are not always like those in the *Friends* series. At home, unconscious forces can take over, often subtly, resulting in one or several people being scape-goated, manipulated, abused or simply misunderstood. As children we have little awareness of such issues and even less choice in the matter. As adults it is important that we do not repeat childhood dynamics and allow people to treat us in ways that may be damaging, since this can make it hard to feel spiritually 'whole' and to practise disciplines such as meditation. These unconscious forces are quite different from the experience of living with people who are grumpy, difficult, demanding or unreliable – failings of which we are all guilty! These matters are subtle but if you are honest with yourself you will know the truth. Can you follow your life path in this home? Can you develop and grow? If the answer is yes, then the chances are you are safe.

picking up negative vibes

Even an essentially healthy home will have its bad atmospheres caused by quarrels and negative emotions that arise within every family and also

from the stresses and strains of life that come in from outside. These hang in the air and are easily picked up by anyone who is sensitive. We are all aware of coming in to an 'atmosphere' when we enter a room where people have been arguing. If a strong emotion persists, the walls and furniture will absorb it. For this reason it is important to be aware of the 'vibe' of any second-hand furniture you might acquire, to ensure that it brings positive vibes to your home.

The ability of cats to relax can be wonderfully therapeutic and will help you unwind.

pet rescue

Pets are often a help when tuning in to atmospheres: dogs tend to be attracted to positive spots and cats to negative ones – hence their penchant for sitting on the laps of cat-haters! However, cats do not *create* what is negative – rather, they are able to neutralize it. Plants also help to cleanse the atmosphere of the home.

Sometimes it is hard to recognize an atmosphere if you have lived with it continually. If you are not quite sure about the atmosphere in your house, go out and clear your mind. When you come back in, notice the effect the house has on you. Try to put this into words, however irrational it may seem at first. If there is unpleasantness, it is better for you to be clear about it as you work to eradicate it (see *Cleansing techniques*).

the effects of personality

Different people have very different effects on a situation. Some individuals cheer you up with a word and a smile, others have a calming presence, while some are disturbing or depressing – it is important to be aware of this.

The person who is the 'life and soul of the party' is not just valued for her jokes and buffoonery but for what she is, for the atmosphere she exudes. Other people, however polite and considerate they may be, simply do not put you at your ease. I have observed this countless times, and each time I wonder if it is just 'me', only to find out later that most other people have the same reaction.

thought and intention

In times gone by, belief in the 'evil eye' was common, and certain people were credited with the ability to cause harm just by looking and ill-wishing. The idea that looking at someone can produce an effect has some basis in fact, since some people are aware, consciously or subconsciously, that someone is staring at them. Very often in a crowd, something will make you turn your head in the direction of a person who is looking at you. We all affect each other by our thoughts and our intentions. How many times has someone popped into your mind only for that person to phone you the next minute? We are connected to others in unseen ways and their feelings are part of the fabric of the world we inhabit.

Take note of who puts you at your ease, regardless of the look on their face.

avoiding envy

To be able to take a compliment gracefully is considered desirable, showing confidence and self-esteem. However, in less sophisticated circles, compliments are regarded with suspicion, denoting envy. In

Being warm and responsive should not make you vulnerable. Always keep a personal space that feels comfortable to you.

primitive societies they may even be dangerous, and beautiful children or treasured possessions may be concealed, not just to prevent physical abduction or theft, but to avoid negative influences resulting from jealousy. Instinctively, we are aware that the thoughts and desires of others impinge upon us.

emotional muddle

From a modern 'psychological' perspective, there are people who do not 'own' parts of their personality and let bits spill out over those close to them. An example might be a very intellectual person who cannot cope with passion and jealousy. He may behave in a detached way, while exuding an inky atmosphere, or withhold affection so that he arouses in the other person the very strong feelings he is at such pains to repress. Then, of course, it is the other person's fault; and thereby hangs a complex tale of emotions getting twisted up so that it is hard to be sure who feels what!

trust your intuition

We all affect the psychic 'climate' around us, and while it is important to acknowledge negative feelings such as envy and resentment, it is best not to feed or project them. By the same token, if someone makes you uneasy, this is something to be taken seriously, since it is not weakness or 'just imagination'. While it is possible that such feelings may arise from our own negativity it is important to protect and distance ourselves from the problematic individual (see *Protection techniques*).

Smile at yourself and be positive about your image – it's a great boost to self-esteem.

self-awareness and honesty

When taking steps to protect yourself it is important to know where the threat originates – it may be coming from you! Without self-awareness, solving life's problems and moving on may be well-nigh impossible. However, it is important to strike a balance, since interpreting everything in terms of our own psychology and its 'pathology' can be very disempowering.

For instance, a woman may waste years working on issues arising from a bad relationship with her father, believing that her current relationship difficulties stem from this and are essentially her fault. In fact, she may be involved with someone who is unsuitable or unpleasant, and she needs to end the relationship, without guilt.

could it be you?

Keeping all of this in mind, we need to ask ourselves how much we are responsible for 'bad' psychic atmospheres. Might *you*, for instance, be the partner with the repressed jealousy, believing it is the fault of the other party for 'causing' these feelings? Who is contaminating whom? Could you possibly be the office bully, making others feel inferior because of your own deep insecurities? Or are you simply paranoid and inadequate, imagining someone is out to 'get' you?

This is where it gets complicated, and the problem is that often the most sensitive, well-meaning people arrive at the conclusion that, yes, it is all their fault, they deserve it, and so the bad situation may continue.

cut to the chase

The ancient Greek conqueror Alexander the Great refused to get bogged down in untying the Gordian Knot and instead slashed through it with his sword! This approach has a great deal of merit when it comes to self-awareness and psychic protection. If you feel threatened you have a right to protect yourself, and that's the bottom line. Also, the methods you use to do this are not designed to harm others and will most likely enhance your self-awareness and spirituality into the bargain.

Jung's ideas about the Shadow may be hard to take, but they are very helpful for psychic awareness.

you and your Shadow

However, if you have some psychic awareness, you will feel much stronger if you get to know yourself and untie some of the knots. Start by being honest with yourself about your true feelings. The unacceptable truth is that we often hate, despise or fear the very things in others that we dislike and repress in ourselves. Jung called this the Shadow archetype, and much unpleasantness in the world results from people trying to destroy 'out there' what they really need to deal with 'inside'.

For instance, say you hate 'selfish' people – not just dislike but have a 'thing' about them. Shadow-matters usually have an extreme quality! The truth may be that you are denying your own selfish side, and maybe there is a part of you that is intensely self-seeking. Perhaps you need to be more consciously selfish, standing up for your own needs in a firm and balanced way. Recognizing your own Shadow can save you psychic energy and prevent you boxing at shadows!

the effects of place

While any place can be filled with an atmosphere by the strong and persistent emotions of people that inhabit it, some spots have an ambience created by influences that are more long-standing and recurrent. These forces are inherent in the place itself, and while human feelings and activity may intensify this, people did not cause it in the first place.

ley lines

Stonehenge in Great Britain and other similar sites have a powerful essence – take note of how this affects you.

There has long been a theory about lines of energy, called ley lines, running across the surface of the Earth's crust. Some people believe that their existence is borne out by a succession of landmarks or tracks, going in a straight line. Standing stones, churches, clumps of trees, wells, beacons and many other features may be found on a straight line on the map. These lines can be detected by dowsers and sensitive people.

Several hypotheses have been put forward to explain these lines, including the assertion that they are imaginary. However, I have experienced the effects of such lines and believe that many can be understood as spirit paths, where there is a mysterious interface between the worlds. Where several lines intersect may be a place of special power. Dowsers identify different types of line, some bringing inspiration, some depression, and in the case of the very worst 'black' lines, unpleasant hauntings, accidents and illness.

If you have your house dowsed by an experienced and competent dowser, he or she may locate lines and neutralize any harmful ones. You may then cleanse your house (see *Cleansing techniques*).

watery impressions

Places where there is water, above or below ground, are most likely to have strong atmospheres. Water seems to hold impressions and spirit sightings in such places are common. Emotions may be imprinted on the water and may have a potent effect on anyone sensitive, and so the atmosphere builds. For example, if someone commits suicide in such a place, this poor soul would leave behind a strong imprint of desperation. If another depressed person comes to the same spot, he or she will 'pick up' on the misery. If you feel you are or have been in such a place, it is a good idea to cleanse and protect yourself.

ghostly presence

Hauntings are most common along ley lines and close to water, and fall into two types. The first type is the 'imprint', where emotions, happy or sad, leave an echo that plays and replays. This may result in sound and even sight, but it is no more than a spirit 'video'. The second type of haunting involves a spirit entity or soul who has not passed on. The sensations aroused by each type are different – in the former case one feels the emotions concerned, but in the latter one is more aware of being intruded upon. I have had many experiences of walking into an empty room and knowing I was not alone. If the presence that you sense is threatening, it is best to leave, but if that is impossible you can cleanse the area and erect a protective magic circle (see *Protection techniques*).

curses and psychic attack

In medieval times few doubted that curses worked. Curses could be passed down through successive generations in a family and objects, too, could be cursed. In Africa, cursing is common and many an unfortunate has given up and died after a witch-doctor has targeted him. Of course, if an individual knows he has been cursed, then it takes no more than his own belief to bring him into decline.

Can one person influence another simply by thought? Experiments by biologist and anthropologist author Lyall Watson (1939–) prove that our thoughts really can affect life-forms around us. I believe that while most 'curses' are little more than suggestion, we certainly can touch others by our projected feelings.

fighting malevolent thoughts

Within day-to-day situations it is not uncommon to be exposed to someone who is malevolent. If you work in an office where you know that someone is willing you to fail, it is possible that you will bring about the thing they desire, through your feelings of stress and unhappiness. This is definitely a matter for psychic protection, because it is important that you discipline and direct your imagination to work for you. However, it is also possible that this person may affect you by their thoughts.

It is important to keep things in proportion and not be paranoid! Most such effects are very small, and a healthy, confident person can and does do the psychic equivalent of brushing them away, often unconsciously. There may be times, however, when you are weakened and vulnerable and this is when stronger action needs to be taken (see *Protection techniques*).

emotional vampires

Certain people may act like emotional vampires. We are all familiar with the kind of person who seems to sap our energy. Sometimes this person may be quite kind and pleasant, and yet after some time in his company all your vitality seems to have seeped out. Other individuals may subtly undermine you with comments, hints and digs that evoke unease. In the first case, the individual may have no idea that he is leaching energy. On a subtle level his aura is feeding off yours because of some need he has. The second case is more sinister, since this person seeks actively to undermine you. In both cases, it is important to stay away, unless and until you feel totally protected.

psychic attack

Finally, there is the unlikely possibility of psychic attack by a practising occultist. This can take several forms, such as sending malevolent thought-forms or attack by a spirit-double. Unless you are deeply involved with occult practices and interact with people who might try this, the possibility of this happening is negligible. If you believe you are subject to this kind of attack, then enlist the support of someone experienced to help you combat it. The routines described in *Protection techniques* will go a long way towards helping.

By developing inward peace and concentration, it is possible to protect yourself on all levels.

energies of the natural world

The beauties of nature can fill you with joy and have a tremendously strengthening effect.

Psychic phenomena tend to be linked with darkened rooms, old buildings and flickering candles. Such things are eerie and psychic senses are often heightened after darkness falls, because of certain chemicals released in the brain. Moonlight, too, stimulates a person's intuition. However, you certainly do not have to wait for nightfall to develop your psychic powers. The wisest and gentlest teacher is all around you in the natural world.

communing with nature

If you wish to become more attuned to the subtle realms, get away from built-up areas to where trees grow and green fields extend into the distance. If you live in the city, then nearby parkland will suffice. Humankind evolved in close communion with nature and in our primitive state our instincts were more highly developed than they are now, insulated as we are by the white noise of civilization. Take regular walks in the countryside. Be aware of the satisfying sensation of your feet upon the Earth, the wind in your hair, the sound of birds and the scent of plant-life all around you. Linger close to trees, examine the flowers. There is no need to do anything but 'be' and enjoy. Nature will do the rest.

nature's psychic energy

There are many specific energies in nature that can help you in the process of psychic protection. Herbs, flowers, trees, scents, crystals, music and drumming – all can serve to change consciousness so that you are more able to sense and to visualize. These objects or sounds also have their own intrinsic qualities that help to alter the subtle climate around you.

using the senses

Smell is the most primitive of the senses, and scent affects the brain-stem and can quickly change the mood. Scent is released when essential oils of plants are heated in an oil-burner or when these oils are massaged into the skin in a carrier oil. Incense is derived from plant materials. Used loose or burnt as a cone or joss stick, incense is a potent way of changing the vibration in a room.

Music, whether a tune or the simple sound of a bell or drum, speaks directly to the instincts and can set a room humming with new and powerful vibration. One of the most uplifting and pure sounds is that of the Tibetan singing bowl – wonderful for cleansing a space.

Crystals and scents not only bring pleasure, they also may be powerful protection tools.

Movement, such as dance, alters the ambience in a room, and touch has an immediate effect on mood. A therapeutic massage can heal and strengthen at a deep level, providing a firm foundation for psychic protection.

crystal energy

Crystals store energy and have healing, pacifying and protecting qualities, giving strength and wisdom. The right crystal can be a friend and companion in life. The specific attributes of crystals are linked to their colour, and colours themselves have the power to influence and change mood and have a positive effect on our health.

your aura

Around each living thing, including us, there is an aura, an emanation of subtle force of many colours that can be seen with practice. The aura of a healthy person may extend around their body for over a metre (about a yard), and spiritual masters are reputed to have auras that are much wider. We pass through the auras of other people regularly, and while we may not be consciously aware of this, it has an effect and is very relevant to psychic protection.

the etheric body

The aura has several layers — many occultists believe that there are seven layers. For practical purposes, however, it is only necessary to recognize two — the innermost layer and the rest. The innermost layer of your aura is called the 'etheric' and it is easy to see. Bluey-grey and extending a couple of centimetres (an inch) around your body, the etheric layer is the energy-body that interpenetrates your physical body, and so is an indication of a person's physical energy and general vigour. The rest of the aura may consist of many different colours and relates to emotions, mentality and spirituality.

Seeing the etheric is simple — look around your fingers or around your whole body in a mirror. When we are little children we readily see our aura, but as we grow we lose this ability. Seeing is believing, but believing is also seeing. Believe that you can see your aura and you will! The best way may be to practise with a friend — ask him or her to stand against a light background and look towards but beyond the person, in an unfocused way. You can also feel your etheric by bringing your palms together and sensing the cushion of energy between them.

a protective shield

An etheric layer that is vibrant and scintillating can throw off harmful influences. The further reaches of your aura may be sensitive to encroachment by anything unpleasant and if you are sufficiently attuned it will act as an early-warning system. In fact, this happens instinctively, making you uneasy or your skin crawl. Without consciously realizing it, you will also be sensing the auras of others. Negative feelings, illness, depression, malevolence or mental imbalance will show in the aura even if they are otherwise concealed. By consciously cleansing your aura regularly, you can keep yourself psychically safe; your aura can be used as a practical working area to create your protective bubble (see *Protection techniques*).

relaxed practice

Practise seeing and sensing auras whenever you feel relaxed. A gently playful state of mind is better for perceiving auras than concentrated staring. Objects also have auras and sometimes these are very powerful as in the case of a treasured possession that has been kept close to the owner and regularly used. A powerful personality can make a strong imprint on an object for good or ill and for this reason care needs to be taken when acquiring anything that has been owned by someone else.

Each of us is surrounded by an aura of light. With a little practice this can be seen.

the chakras

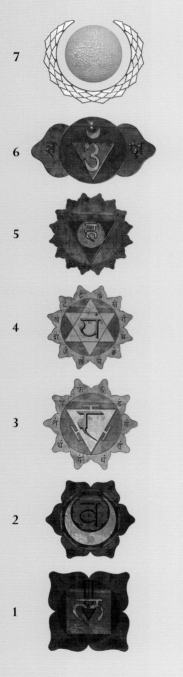

7

6

5

4

3

2

1

A Sanskrit word meaning 'wheel', a *chakra* is an energy centre in the body. The seven major chakras represent the organs in the subtle body, and when operating efficiently, they spin round; when blocked the chakras may become sluggish, which will have an effect on a person's wellbeing. Soundly functioning chakras are important for psychic strength and personal power.

the seven major chakras

Although there are many minor chakras in the body, the seven major ones run in a vertical line from the top of the head to the base of the spine. Awakening the chakras is part of the process of spiritual enlightenment, and it is necessary to be aware of the seven chakras for the purposes of psychic protection.

The seven major chakras follow the seven colours of the rainbow, although some occultists say this is now changing and that most people's chakras are colour-free. My awareness of them is still based on colours and this is a good way of beginning to attune to their meanings.

1 **The base chakra** is situated at the base of the spine, close to the genitals and the anus and is associated with the colour red. This chakra draws energy up from the Earth and the surrounding ether into the body. It needs to be working well for the basic functioning of the body and the other chakras, for it is literally 'the base'. A feeble base chakra can result in you feeling 'spaced out' and out of synch with people and surroundings.

2 **The sacral chakra** is approximately a hand's breadth below your navel. It is orange and is connected with your sex-drive, emotional nature and creative energy. If it isn't working properly relationships suffer because we are not able to accept our own needs and sense those of others. By the same token, we find it hard to meet the needs of another. If this chakra is impaired we can feel insecure, anxious and panicky.

3 **The solar plexus chakra** is between the navel and breastbone. It is golden yellow and relates to emotions, self-esteem and personal power.

This chakra is our internal 'sun', giving us individuality and willpower. If it does not 'shine' brightly we may let others dominate us, feeling afraid to express an opinion or insist on our rights. The solar plexus chakra is especially important in psychic protection, because it is a power-source that can radiate around you.

4 **The heart chakra** is in the middle of the chest. It is green and is the centre of loving feelings. Here is the site of true compassion and identification with others. While this is about very human love, it is also the starting-point for links with the Divine. The heart chakra can be activated by mystical responses to nature. If this chakra is not working properly it may result in a person who is emotionally withholding. However, if the heart chakra is too open, for too long, it will result in depletion and exhaustion. This is what can happen if we allow ourselves to be too responsive, helpful and 'sorry for people'.

5 **The throat chakra** is, not surprisingly, situated in the throat. It is blue and rules your ability to communicate thoughts and feelings and is also connected to music. This chakra relates to the power of the voice and if functioning well enables you to speak ringingly. A poorly functioning throat chakra results in misunderstandings and the inability to voice feelings. Sometimes problems with this chakra manifest as sore throats and may be physical evidence that we are not able to get through to others. When the chakra is cleared, so are the problems.

6 **The brow chakra** is in the centre of the brow, on the 'third eye' or psychic centre. It is coloured indigo and relates to insight, inspiration, intuition and imagination. If this chakra is working well then the intellect functions in a clear and balanced way. We also feel 'in tune' and that we can 'see' the truth. When the brow chakra is blocked, then we can become hidebound, unable to see the wood for the trees and incapable of lateral or original thinking. Headaches may also result.

7 **The crown chakra** is on the top of the head and is violet. It is also the site of the 'many-petalled lotus' that blooms with light. This is a very spiritual centre and it can feel disturbing if anyone gets too close or touches you there, especially if you do not like the person. This chakra is a connection to the higher realms and a beacon for spiritual development. If the crown chakra is blocked, depression and a sense of meaninglessness can result.

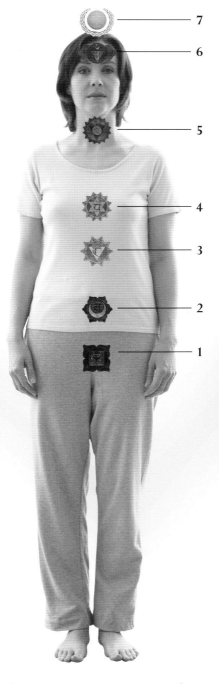

The seven major chakras run in a vertical column through the centre of the body.

the major chakras

	CHAKRA	POSITION IN BODY	COLOUR
	Crown	Top of the head	Violet and white
	Brow	Between eyes	Indigo
	Throat	Neck	Blue
	Heart	Centre of chest	Green; rose pink
	Solar plexus	Below the sternum	Yellow
	Sacral	Hand-breadth below the navel	Orange
	Base	Perineum	Red

GLAND	PARTS OF BODY	EMOTIONAL CONNECTIONS
Pituitary	Upper brain; right eye	Connection with higher self
Pineal	Lower brain; left eye; ear, nose and throat; nervous system	Idealism and intuition
Thyroid; parathyroid	Larynx	Communication and self-expression
Thymus	Heart; lungs; immune system; vagus nerve	Compassion
Pancreas	Stomach; liver; gall bladder	Physical emotions
Gonads	Reproductive system; urinary tract; lower back	Creativity and imagination
Adrenals	Base of spine; rectum and bowel; bone marrow; kidneys	Emotional and physical balance

STRENGTHENING

Some of the advice given in this chapter is common sense; however, common sense is not that common! It is easy to get into bad habits. Without noticing, you can become depleted, and before you know where you are you are faced with something or someone that you find hard to cope with. A few good strengthening practices will ensure that your batteries are always charged.

Evolve a gentle routine that works for you. Although routine is one of those boring words, a good routine is like ritual. The purpose of ritual is to get through to the unconscious mind, which has a childlike simplicity (and we all know how children 'need routine'). A routine does not restrict you, it cradles you, giving life a framework. Once your routine is in place you will automatically eat, exercise, relax and sleep much better. Of course, routine should be flexible, but ensure any breaks are temporary. Flow back into your routine as water into a safe container.

Organization is also vital, so give some thought to structuring your day, building in time for relaxing activities, such as yoga, and for exercise. Tidying is a ritual, so try to keep your home reasonably tidy and clutter-free, since this encourages positive energies to flow and enables you to think clearly. Set aside part of the day for yourself, where you can allow your mind to drift. Early morning or last thing at night may be best for this, and it is essential if you need to be creative or inspired. Take care of life's details and bigger issues will take care of themselves!

taking care of basics

Food should nuture body and spirit — eating is a celebration of life.

Your body is your temple – care for it and your defences will be strong. Check these fundamentals to ensure you really are doing the best for yourself physically, and remember that the mental, emotional and physical form one interdependent unit.

nutrition

Food is a controversial issue for many people: never has it been so plentiful, so varied or so contaminated; obesity is prevalent and diets are an obsession. Please do not diet! Fad diets can be harmful and will weaken you and disrupt your metabolism. It may work in the short-term but in the long run dieting causes cravings, the yo-yo effect, depression, loss of self-esteem and the sad but inevitable weight gain that comes from a body desperately going into starvation mode and laying down more fat.

Instead, choose healthy, locally grown organic foods, make or grow as much as you can and be especially careful of meat that has been cruelly reared. Organize yourself so that you always have healthy food available. Eat regularly. Relax and enjoy your food, giving thanks for the lives that have been given to feed yours.

water

Drink plenty of water – eight glasses a day is the recommended amount. Many physical complaints are due to dehydration. It cleanses and refreshes you physically and psychically, since water molecules carry 'memories' of the Earth. Choose mineral or at least filtered water and leave your water in sunlight for a few minutes to 'charge it up' with energy. Keep water by you, so you can sip regularly.

drugs

Although the effects of alcohol are worse than many other drugs, it is 'culturally contained'. It is a predictably destructive and damaging drug when taken in excess. Other drugs are more unpredictable; all exact a price from the body, even analgesics and prescription drugs. Herbs have the advantage of being natural and so on the same 'wavelength' as your body, but they should be treated with respect since some herbs can kill.

If you are in need of psychic protection, all drugs are totally taboo apart from essential prescription drugs or a glass or two of wine, taken with friends to unwind. Alcohol can weaken your etheric and even allow entities to attach themselves to your aura, so take no chances.

exercise

However busy you are, exercise is essential for a healthy life. It speeds up the metabolism and releases feel-good endorphins into your body, making you feel much more energetic afterwards. It is a great mood-lifter and general strengthener. Find the exercise that you like best – dancing, walking, going to the gym – and organize your life so that you fit it in.

sleep

Our sleep requirements differ hugely – recognize your own sleep needs and meet them. Evolve a bed-time routine that suggests 'sleep' to your brain. Ensure your pillows and bedclothes are the best possible and that your bedroom is airy and secure. *Cleansing techniques* covers cleansing the bedroom, while *Protection techniques* gives hints for psychic safety when sleeping. If your sleep-bank is depleted you are more likely to imagine the worst. However busy you are, allow yourself enough sleep.

Exercise strengthens both your mind and body, and should be an enjoyable activity.

relaxation

Moving from a period of activity into one of quiet involves a change of consciousness and this is helped by little rituals. Create your own winding-down rituals – tidy the house, have a bath or sit by candlelight with a soothing, hot drink, allowing the day to ebb away. If you establish this transition ritual into 'relaxation mode', it will work even when times are especially busy or stressful.

learning to relax

If you experience a stressful episode during the day, allow yourself some time out. Go where you will be alone and concentrate on how your body feels, to ground you. Close your eyes and listen to the sounds around you. Let them recede into the distance. Imagine you are inside a bubble, insulated and safe. If you fall asleep for a moment it does not matter. When you come back to the everyday, clap your hands and affirm that you are returning, refreshed and sharp.

Tension is the greatest barrier between us and the vast sea of cosmic power that flows around us. It will greatly help your abilities to visualize, meditate, feel in contact with higher beings and go through activities such as opening your chakras if you can relax.

Learn to relax by developing a routine of practice, preferably at the same time each day, to get the message into your subconscious. Ten minutes a day is far better than an hour or two once a week. To start, lie down on your bed, for that immediately suggests deep relaxation. Once you have mastered relaxation, then it may be best to move to a chair or lying or sitting on the floor to prevent you falling deeply asleep.

Once you have learned to relax, you will possess a powerful weapon. However tense you may be, take a moment simply to imagine that you are 'doing your relaxation' and your conditioned responses will ensure that any tension drains away, leaving you serene and able to cope with whatever is thrown at you.

Tension is a barrier to psychic power. Realize that yours isn't helping you and let it go.

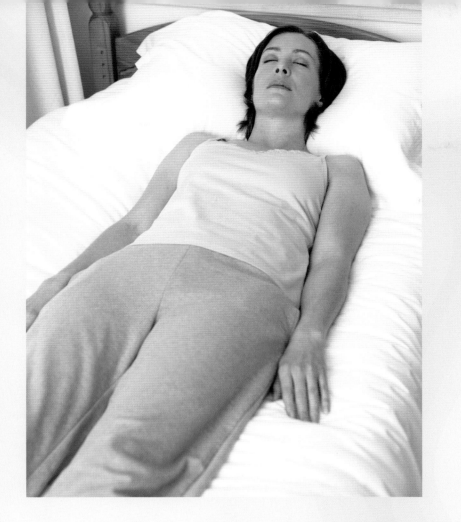

a simple relaxation technique

1 Lie on your bed or on the floor, or if you prefer sit comfortably in a chair or on the floor. Make sure that you will not be disturbed.

2 When you are settled, concentrate on your body. Are there any areas of tension? Bring your awareness into your body and try to relax each area in turn.

3 Imagine that warm water is flowing over you, starting at your crown, going down over the back of your neck, shoulders, arms, hand and fingers. Imagine the water washing down your chest and back, stomach and pelvis and down your legs to your ankles, heels, feet and toes. Repeat this several times, if you like.

4 If thoughts come into your mind, do not fight them. Instead, imagine they are butterflies fluttering in and out again, or that they are flickering across a TV screen. Concentrate on your body and its comfort.

5 An alternative method is to tense each muscle as much as you can, then let it go limp. Start at the crown and work down and up again. This tensing and relaxing releases certain chemicals in the body that are helpful. Or imagine that your limbs are powered by little men, who are downing tools and walking out. Experiment with ways that work for you.

T'ai Chi and Chi Kung

Mind and body form a continuum – what affects one affects the other. It is easy to forget physical matters when involved in the psychic, but a strong and well-functioning body is vital if you are to maximize psychic powers. T'ai Chi and Chi Kung can help promote balance, poise and a sense of being grounded that is vital to a healthy body and mind.

benefits of exercise

Regular exercise keeps your body in good condition and enhances your mood. One of the most important effects of exercise with regard to psychic protection is that it improves your posture and enables you to move in a more fluid, effective way. Holding yourself correctly and moving gracefully are important for several reasons. Firstly, when your posture is good, your body is sending feel-good messages to your brain, telling you that you are confident, serene and prepared for action. Secondly, similar messages are sent to anyone who is near you, through your self-assured body language. Thirdly, you are, in fact, sending out signals to the Universe that you are in tune with your surroundings, attracting positive energies and innately balanced.

The Yin Yang symbol represents cosmic balance and shows any extreme carries the seed of its opposition.

This third factor is perhaps the most subtle, yet the most basic and is at the heart of the physical arts of T'ai Chi and Chi Kung. Taoism, which dates back to 1122 BCE, is at the heart of these practices. Taoism is a spiritual path of oneness with nature and of balance. It is this 'balance' that gives strength, and consists of Yin and Yang, the passive and the assertive, being in equilibrium.

a healing and fighting art

T'ai Chi is a system of moving meditation/martial art which creates external and internal equilibrium, bringing Yin and Yang into harmony. As both a healing and a fighting art, T'ai Chi emphasizes the mind-body connection and focuses on developing the ability to centre oneself and therefore not be easily distracted or confused. The flowing movements of T'ai Chi help to reduce stress and bestow a subtle assurance that sends out signals to others. It is clear that while you are not posing a threat, you possess a serene invincibility.

ancient exercise

Chi Kung is an ancient Chinese exercise, again thousands of years old, but it has continued to be practised widely throughout China and other parts of the world. It is similar to T'ai Chi in that it combines stillness or gentle movement with calm and regular breathing. The movements are simple, but when co-ordinated with proper breathing, the vitality of the body is greatly enhanced, improving health and increasing resistance to disease.

While these methods have an ancient pedigree, much benefit can also be obtained from many New Age Western methods, where dance and movement are used to express feelings and alter mental states. Almost any form of controlled and sensible bodywork will enable you to become more grounded, balanced and assured. As your body harmonizes with your mind, you harmonize with the Cosmos. This essential poise is a very strong basis for psychic protection.

Moving with poise and grace sends out messages of confidence and unites mind and body.

yoga

The earliest written accounts of yoga date from between 1500 and 1200 BCE, but it had existed as an oral tradition from at least a millennium earlier. Yoga's more profound applications take many years and extreme dedication to perfect: however, it can be used to achieve relaxation, harmony and poise.

The word yoga comes from the same Indo-European root as the English verb 'yoke', and it can also mean 'unity' and 'identification'. The union achieved is that of the individual soul with cosmic consciousness. On a more practical level, it also signifies the union of body and mind. The unity of all life is learned on the path of yoga through a programme of practical exercises.

Hatha yoga

Although there are several types of yoga, the one most commonly taught in the West is Hatha yoga – the yoga of health and bodily control. It enables you to understand and feel in command of your body through physical exercises, breathing and hygiene, all of which are based on deep wisdom and knowledge of how the body functions. Yoga does not just exercise and develop muscles but also promotes the health and efficiency of the internal organs, such as the heart, lungs, glands and nervous system. Because the positions (*asanas*) act upon the endocrine glands, they prolong youth and vigour. A healthy mind in a healthy body forms the foundation for spiritual advancement.

Many people find strength, peace and encouragement through the practice of yoga.

using the life-force

Yoga utilizes the life-force (*prana*) inherent within nature to boost health and vigour. The *asanas* are postures to be held, not

exercises as such, and most gently stretch the spine, affecting the nervous system. Routine yoga practice results in the relief of stress and a serene outlook. The shape of your body may improve and if you need to lose weight, this may happen. Yoga confers suppleness, good posture and shapeliness. In addition, there are many mental and emotional benefits – optimism, concentration, zest for life, a benevolent attitude, heightened awareness and the ability to see things in perspective.

The gentle strengthening involved in yoga benefits the circulation and nervous system.

join a class

Yoga is easily practised in a small space, but it is far better to join a regular class. This will give you the grounding and support that you need, and you can get into a routine of daily practice on your own. Yoga is very popular and it is not hard to find a teacher.

Yoga is a powerful tool when used in pursuit of psychic protection. The wisdom in which it is rooted carries the authority of millennia and your subconscious mind will register this. The mental tranquillity achieved through yoga tends to deter aggressors, for they sense they are unlikely to get very far. In addition, it helps you to deal with any threats in a serene and detached manner. The poise and subtle physical strength given by yoga send out signals to others that you are balanced and in command.

Whatever your spiritual beliefs and whatever psychic protection techniques you choose, yoga practice will enhance their effectiveness.

body language

We may believe that it takes time to get to know someone, but in fact we make up our minds in the first few moments. At least 80 per cent of what we need to know about a newcomer is conveyed to us by their appearance, mannerisms and a thousand subtle signals such as posture and stance. All this forms part of body language.

If you are intuitive and observant you will be instantly aware of your reaction to a person, consciously noting the direct or shifty gaze, or the angle of the shoulders. Even if you only notice these things subconsciously, they will affect you and the way you react to the individual. Clearly, body language is eloquent and learning to convey what you want in this way is invaluable in psychic protection.

mastering your own body language

Ensure that your body language expresses warmth and confidence at the start of an encounter.

If your body language is confident and poised, then you are sending out signals that you can handle life and that you are strong. Bullies will move on and troublemakers will feel they may get more than they bargain for.

The best way to send out confident signals is to feel confident. Imagine you have just been paid a massive compliment, told you are doing a fabulous job, that you are capable, successful, going places. When you concentrate on those feelings your shoulders square, your back straightens, your chin tilts and a smile plays around your lips.

Practise in the mirror if you like, and imagine as vividly as you can. Set aside five minutes a day to do this and after a couple of weeks you will be able to switch it on at will. Whenever you need to look confident, imagine the compliments and your body will mould itself into shape.

Your relaxed, erect body tells your brain that you are full of confidence. In return, your brain obliges by actually experiencing confidence, sending more messages to your body to stand tall, and so the positive loop intensifies. The best way to achieve powerful body language is to generate that power from within.

Practising a confident stance in front of a mirror will work wonders for your self-esteem.

positive body language check-list

The following suggestions may help when visualization and imagination have deserted you.

- Relax. Relax your shoulders, arms, face, and smile gently. Do not fidget, shift from foot to foot or bite your nails.

- Stand tall. Imagine there is a string joining your feet to the top of your head and that string is being pulled taut by an imaginary puppeteer.

- Keep your shoulders straight (but relaxed).

- Make direct eye-contact with the person to whom you are speaking, but do not stare them out.

- Smile openly.

- Move slowly – the confident have no need to rush.

- When sitting, keep arms and legs in an open position, which suggests a confidence that has no need to close and conceal.

- Avoid belligerent gestures, such as finger-wagging, jabbing and pointing.

- If someone is aggressive, maintain your confident stance but avoid too much eye-contact, as that may appear challenging. Remaining dignified and reasonable asserts your superiority without being unduly provocative.

strength through contact with nature

Spending time with nature will have a positive effect on your mind, body and spirit.

If you wish to strengthen yourself, seek out the benefits of nature in a systematic way. Any activity outside in the fresh air is a great help towards psychic strength. Gardening is wonderful, since growing things send out so much positive energy and practical confirmation of the powers of Life.

get outside

When you feel stressed, try to get outside where you can place your feet on the earth for a while, to ground you. Take your shoes off if you wish and allow the energies of the Earth to bring you a tonic. Take deep breaths while affirming that you are being cleansed and empowered. Stamp your feet on the ground three times, saying, 'It is gone, I am free, I am whole.'

The strength of Mother Earth is inexhaustible. Draw on her and remember to give back by caring for the Earth, plants and animals in some way. Such caring is a further act of strengthening.

drawing sustenance from trees

1 Go for regular long walks. Look for a special tree that you feel drawn to, then sit with your back to the tree and become aware of its essence. Relax and feel yourself surrounded by the aura of the tree, safe and secure.

2 Think about the roots of the tree, penetrating deep within the Earth. Imagine that you also are growing roots from your feet that reach down into the soil. Become aware of the richness of the earth, and all the dark, secret places into which your roots are penetrating.

3 Now feel yourself drawing sustenance up through these roots. The profound essence of Mother Earth, and all the energies that have nurtured life throughout millions of years, are seeping up into you. Like the tree you are strong, wise, steadfast. Your body feels full of energy. You know the truth of the seasons, coming and going in endless cycle. All things come into perspective and are powerless to affect you in any serious way. Rooted in Mother Earth and sheltered by the tree you are impregnable.

4 When you are ready, feel your roots shrinking back, receding from the deep heart of the soil until they are re-absorbed into your feet. Thank the tree for its shelter. Pat your body to make sure you are totally back to normal. You can repeat this exercise every day if you wish. It is very grounding and will give you a serene stability.

opening and closing your chakras

In order to function at your best physically and spiritually, each chakra needs to be working properly, neither blocked nor leaking energy from your body-spirit system. Learning to open your chakras will put you in touch with their functioning and will stimulate and clear them. You will be able to energize yourself and raise your level of spiritual awareness, which is useful if you feel under psychic bombardment, giving you the strength to combat negativity.

Imagine each closed chakra is like a flower with tightly closed petals after a rain storm.

Before beginning any work on your chakras look back to pages 28–31 to familiarize yourself with their purposes, locations and colours within the body. Opening your chakras is a good precursor to any spiritual activity, such as meditating, visualizing and doing the exercises for protection, positive energies and blessing given in the following chapters, *Protection techniques*, *Drawing positive energies* and *Advanced matters*. It increases awareness at all levels, can enhance your power and will boost your general health and wellbeing.

If a chakra feels hard to open or less vibrant than the others, then it may be blocked or sluggish. Using the suggestions on page 47 concentrate on it for a bit longer, imagining it strengthening and brightening. Remember, opening your chakras is a potent step into the subtle realms, helping you to master the energies within you, en route to the energies outside. It will make you feel strong and alive, and the technique is worth taking the trouble to perfect.

opening your chakras

Choose a time and a place when you won't be disturbed. Choose a place that is free of any disturbance – physical, mental, emotional or spiritual – and avoid overhead power-cables, machinery and technology, discordant people or any location that has an unpleasant 'feel'. Make sure you know the position and colour of each chakra (see pages 30–31).

1 Lie down, preferably on your bed, and go into a relaxed state (see Relaxation, pages 36–37). Feel peaceful and serene.

2 Turn your attention to your base chakra. Imagine its vibrant red colour. Think about its qualities of strength and survival, and relish how it connects you to your roots and to Mother Earth. Imagine energy rising from the Earth and entering this chakra, energizing it and filling it with vibrancy. As this is the first chakra and your first attempt, do not be in a hurry. Opening chakras is easy, but because we have placed so many barriers to our perception of subtle matters, it may take a while before you feel anything has happened. Enjoy what you are doing, take a light-hearted approach and remain relaxed.

3 When your chakra opens you may feel flooded with colour, light and energy. Your body may twitch; you may feel as if you are floating; or you may feel very sexy! On the other hand, any sensations you experience may be very mild. Do not talk yourself out of anything you are feeling – it is not 'just imagination'. Your experience will be unique to you, whatever form it takes.

4 Once you feel your base chakra has opened, it is relatively simple to open the others. However, on the first few attempts it may be best to stay with the base chakra, working on this and ensuring that you have opened it thoroughly, before proceeding to any of the higher chakras.

5 Once you feel reasonably confident that your base chakra is open, you can proceed to the next chakra. Draw the power up from your base chakra and feel it enter the sacral chakra, energizing it. Think about the qualities of this chakra and its glowing wonderful orange colour. Reflect on all the positive aspects of your sexuality and how good it is to be part of the stream of life. It is important to think only positive thoughts, so if anything negative intrudes, concentrate simply on the colour and the chakra. Feel a surge of energy as it opens.

6 Now draw the power up to your solar plexus chakra. It is as if the Sun is shining within you! Feel confident and expansive, full of radiance. Reflect on your creativity and talents (remember, only positives). Delight in this chakra for a few moments.

7 When you are ready, proceed to your heart chakra. As the green colour floods you, you may feel overcome by love for the world and all of nature. Or your experience may be of love in different manifestations. This is pure, giving, radiating love. Concentrate on this for a few minutes.

8 Draw the power further upwards to your throat chakra. Be aware of its celestial blue. Realize what an asset you possess in your powers of communication. At this point you may hear music or hear voices.

9   Now draw the energy up into your brow or third eye chakra. As its rich indigo permeates you, realize that your awareness can and will expand, making you wise and insightful.

10 And so to the crown chakra, with its pure violet, opening you to the meanings within life and beyond. This can be an inexpressibly uplifting experience.

11 Be aware now that the power is issuing from your crown like a shining fountain. Direct it downwards, back into your solar plexus chakra. Continue this for a short while, strengthening the power-circuit so you are really 'humming', like a battery. This will strengthen your willpower and individuality. You should feel joyful, strong and energized. At this point you can put the chakras 'into the background' as it were, and get on with your visualization, or spiritual activity. Your conviction, awareness and power will increase every time you open your chakras.

closing down your chakras

You must always close down your chakras with care, even if you are not sure that you have opened them. If you have only consciously opened your base chakra, still visualize closing them all, just in case. This is very important. Open chakras can make you vulnerable, light-headed, subject to migraine, nervousness and bad-temper, so ensure you close them properly.

1 Close down your chakras by imagining each one in turn as a flower upon which heavy rain is falling, flowing downwards, make all their petals close tightly. Or imagine they are eyes, closing.

2 Affirm strongly that each chakra is closed.

3 It is important that you go over this thoroughly in your mind. Carry on doing it for a while, even after you feel sure your chakras are closed. This becomes easier with practice.

4 Once you have come back to the everyday world, eat or drink something (not just water), touch the ground with your palms to ground yourself and give yourself time to adjust.

CLEANSING TECHNIQUES

Psychic hygiene is very important for psychic protection. If you are inwardly 'cleansed' then it is more difficult for negativity to attach to you and easier to recognize when this has happened. Likewise at home; a home that has a clear atmosphere is much nicer to return to: it will help you to shed all the aggravation of the day and will radiate protection. Before placing protective shields around yourself and your home, however, you want to be sure that you aren't locking in negativity.

Psychic cleansing isn't a one-off practice. Cleansing rituals are powerful and effective ways of ridding yourself of anything harmful, and should be repeated at intervals and whenever you feel the need. This is a pleasant thing to do, making you feel uplifted and attuned to the beauty of life.

Repression is not the same as 'cleansing'; there is no need to smother your negative emotions in order to be spiritual. Spirituality does not arise from what you feel but from what you choose to do with those feelings. Be honest with yourself and then you can be in control. It may help to write down on paper the unwanted feelings and then burn it in a heat-proof container. Be prepared to do this as many times as necessary.

When dispelling any negativity or emotion, imagine that it is going somewhere specific, otherwise it could return. Visualize it going into the Earth to be neutralized and transformed, or up towards the Sun where it will be cleansed and returned to the cosmic energy-pool. It has gone from you and the Universe has accepted it.

cleansing yourself

A bath can cleanse you spiritually, psychically and be a very enjoyable experience too.

One of the simplest ways to cleanse yourself psychically (as well as physically) is to have a bath. Light some candles and place a few drops of lavender oil in your bath-water. As you lie in the bath, imagine all those unwanted feelings and troublesome thoughts seeping out of you into the water.

As you pull the plug, affirm that all the bad stuff is going down the drain. You can also use a shower, which may be more invigorating. Whenever you take a bath or shower, incorporate this visualization, however briefly.

smudging

Your aura picks up negativity from your surroundings and also from your own emotions. One pleasant way to cleanse your aura derives from Native American tradition and involves passing a smouldering bundle of dried sage and sweet-grass through and around the aura until it is pure and clear. Smudge sticks are easy to obtain in New Age shops, and they are best used with a partner or friend, each person taking it in turn to cleanse the other.

visualization

Another way to cleanse your aura is to sit on a chair with both feet firmly on the ground, close your eyes and imagine that there is a large shower nozzle above your head. From the nozzle visualize a thick, wide stream of golden particles covering and streaming through your aura, leaving it sparkling and vibrant. Imagine the total extent of your aura being cleansed, and continue for a while, even when you think you have completed the task. Visualize all the negativity flowing into the Earth beneath your feet and being neutralized.

breathing

You can cleanse your aura by breathing. Imagine that the boundary of your aura is a membrane that lets the unwanted escape and then seals itself against harmful things. Everything negative that you have absorbed is being emitted in your breath – see it as grey smoke that you are expelling. Breathe deeply and concentrate on blowing out everything harmful through your auric sheath (the sheath that encloses all the individual energies of an entity – in this case you). You can carry on breathing and blowing until you feel cleansed, then do it for a little while longer. Be careful not to hyperventilate.

This method is especially good when your own emotions have been aroused. If you feel that fear or anger have lodged in part of your body, often in the solar plexus, stroke this energy out of your aura. You will feel it as a knot or 'fuzziness'. Ease this out with your hands. As you do so the feeling may intensify, so just let yourself experience it and continue what you are doing, letting go and imagining that you are directing this energy into a hole in the ground. When you are ready, mentally close the hole and ask that it be turned into 'compost', eventually to fertilize new life.

If it feels right, you can combine several of these approaches. Do not expect to feel squeaky-clean immediately, but soon you will feel light and free.

Cleanse your aura by sitting peacefully, while imagining it to be purified of all negativity.

cleansing your home

The current habit of neglecting housework is not good psychic practice; if there is clutter and mess around, then *chi* or life energy becomes stagnant and the dirty house is more likely to hold on to negative energies.

You do not have to go mad with bleach and polish in order to have a clean house. If a house is tidy, then keeping it reasonably clean takes very little time. Get rid of old newspapers, empty bins daily, put things away after you use them and whisk round quickly with a duster and a vacuum cleaner. As you do this you are giving out a message to yourself and to the Cosmos that you are master in your own home.

Cleansing your home physically with a besom means you are also cleansing it psychically.

psychic spring clean

Use a besom broom, which symbolizes magic and movement, to psychically cleanse your house. It is best to cleanse a house thoroughly before you move in, but if this isn't possible, you can do it when all the furniture is in place. Starting with the room furthest from the door, sweep all negativity out with the besom, imagining it as grey clouds being driven out by your broom. When you have thoroughly swept one room, close the door and proceed to the next. When all the rooms on one floor are cleansed, sweep the bad energies into a ball and continue until you have accumulated all negativity in one big grey pile. Then open the front door and sweep it out, asking the Earth to take care of it.

spiritual cleansing

Now cleanse your house spiritually with the power of the four elements. Equip a tray with a lighted candle, a lavender joss stick, a bowl of salt and a chalice of water, symbolizing the elements Fire, Air, Earth and Water, respectively. Again, start in the remotest room. Stand in the centre of the room and take the joss stick round the room anti-clockwise, saying,

'Be cleansed by Air'. Follow this with the candle, saying, 'Be cleansed by Fire'; then carry the chalice around the room, sprinkling drops around and saying, 'Be cleansed by Water', and finally move around sprinkling the salt with the words 'Be cleansed by Earth'.

Now perform the same actions clockwise, saying, 'Be blessed by Air' and so on. Pay special attention to important areas such as your beds, the dining table, a favourite chair. Finally, in an anti-clockwise fashion, go around as much of the perimeter of your house as you can to cleanse it; follow this clockwise to bless it, with each of the elements in the same order as before (Air, Fire, Water, Earth). Where you cannot get around the side of the house, stand and imagine or do it internally.

You can repeat this at intervals, perhaps at turning points in the year, such as New Year or in the spring. Regularly light candles or burn joss sticks to recharge the air and open windows frequently. This type of cleansing is a necessary preliminary to sealing and protecting (see *Protection techniques*).

Air, Water, Earth and Fire assembled make a statement of both beauty and serenity.

cleansing with sound

Sound is vibration and is a potent tool for cleansing. Simple clapping, bells, wind-chimes, Tibetan singing bowls, musical instruments and the human voice can all be used to refresh the energy in a room.

Wind-chimes are visually as well as audially appealing, so hang yours where there is a breeze.

clapping and bell-ringing

Wherever you feel negative energy, clap in staccato bursts to bring an end to what is hanging around. A bell is also good for this; take time choosing your 'cleansing' bell, finding one that has the clear, silvery tone that seems right for you. Take the bell around your house, office, car or any other area that needs to be psychically cleansed. Ring it in every corner, moving it up, down and towards the door.

wind-chimes and singing bowls

Wind-chimes are wonderful for keeping the subtle atmosphere fresh and clean. Site these wherever they can pick up a draught. Like bells, wind-chimes need to be chosen carefully for the sound they make – while wooden chimes have their own uses in creating ambience, metallic ones may be better for cleansing.

Most wonderful of all is a Tibetan singing bowl. Again, choose carefully since there is a knack to making the bowl 'sing'. The sound is not only cleansing but very uplifting, significantly raising the vibrations of any place. It is a wonderful precursor to any spiritual practice, ritual or meditation.

Playing a musical instrument will purify and enrich the atmosphere. Music that you choose makes a place 'yours' and it is good to play it as much as possible.

Classical or New Age music may be the best choice for purification, but no self-respecting spook will hang around for long if you play a burst of pop music. The most important thing is to go with your instincts.

use your voice

The human voice is very powerful because it has so many tones and is directed by your will. One of the most useful things you can do when cleansing any area is to chant, which helps to change your consciousness and also the character of your surroundings. One chant could be:

Cleansed be, safe be
All badness flee from me.

Repeat this as you ritually 'sweep' a room or brush out a car. A longer chant, adapted from Wiccan ceremonies goes:
Broom of wood, so true and strong,
Free me and mine from any wrong,
All that's dark now put to flight,
Cleanse this space and let in light!

This can be sung to the tune of 'Frere Jacques', repeating 'Let in light!' as the chorus. Sing it over and over as many times as you like. By all means invent your own chants or change the words to a favourite tune to suit your purposes. Use the power of your voice to ring out a message on the subtle planes.

Few sounds are more cleansing and uplifting than that of a Tibetan singing bowl.

Finally, there are very few things that brighten an atmosphere at all levels better than laughter, so lighten up, put a smile on your face and see that laughter is the best medicine.

cleansing with scent

Scent is the most primitive of our senses, involving the reptilian brain-stem, that most instinctual part of our brain. Scent has the ability to change consciousness rapidly and deeply because it works on this instinctual level. Herbs and flowers give off their own individual scents and each of these has traditional meanings and uses. Be guided by these, but always go with what feels right to you.

incense

There are several ways of creating scent for the purposes of ritual cleansing. One method is to use incense, which is made of dried plant materials – essential oils dripped on these may enhance their fragrance. You need incense, a censer and disc-shaped charcoal, all of which are usually found in New Age shops. Hold the charcoal in tongs and light one side in a candle flame, until it sparkles. Place it in the censer and sprinkle incense in the little dip in the disc – the charcoal is to heat the incense. Magical fragrance will coil into the air and you can waft this around the area in question. (Note: Please get a proper container in which to burn your incense – an old ashtray will not do as it could crack!)

Let the spiritual power of the scent from joss sticks lift you to another level of experience.

Joss sticks are a form of solid incense, shaped somewhat like a chopstick. They are very convenient, although their ingredients are not always reliable and some smell awful!

Essential oils are a simple non-messy way to create a powerful ambience in a room.

essential oils

Burning incense is marvellous for a focused ritual but a good choice for creating a pleasant ambience is an essential oil warmed in an oil-burner. The burner heats water in which a few drops of essential oil are placed, so releasing mild fragrance over an extended period. Essential oils are extracted from the essence of plants, and although most are gentle, some can be strong and need to be treated with respect. Be careful of allergies and damage to surfaces in the home.

ESSENTIAL OIL	PROPERTIES AND USES
Lavender	As incense or oil this is a cleanser second-to-none. Gentle and will not harm the skin. Make your own lavender incense by drying lavender-heads.
Cedarwood	Fragrant, purifying and protective, enhances spirituality, creates peace, dispels stagnation.
Cypress	Eases grief and bereavement and clears the path for change.
Eucalyptus	Excellent for healing.
Frankincense	Majestic and uplifting, heightens awareness, dispels old traumas.
Lemon balm (Melissa)	Cleanses away bad emotions, soothes the spirit, aids sleep.
Myrrh	Gets rid of negativity and stuck-in-a-rut feelings. Fights lethargy and despondency.
Orange	Brings energy, optimism and decisiveness.
Patchouli	Great for protection and grounding.
Peppermint	A strongly purifying and energizing oil.
Rosemary	Clears the head, revives and freshens, aids memory.
Sage	Dispels depression, aids memory.
Tea Tree	Not the pleasantest scent, but strongly purifying, stimulating and antiseptic.
Thyme	Releases blockages and past traumas.
Ylang ylang	Drives away troublesome feelings such as jealousy. Lifts obsession, brings peace and bliss.

BLEND	FOR A SPECIFIC PURPOSE
Myrrh, frankincense, cedar	Banish a bad atmosphere; lopsided aura.
Cedar, rosemary	General purification.
Myrrh, ylang ylang, rosemary	Banish emotional strife.
Frankincense, cedar, patchouli	Protection.
Orange and frankincense	Brightness and happiness.

cleansing with dance and movement

Dance harmonizes body, mind and spirit, and connects the human soul to the energies of the Cosmos, similar to Chi Kung and T'ai Chi (see pages 38–39). Dancing and movement can be natural and instinctual, following the impulse of the moment and a response to music. If you love to dance, by doing so you are creating very positive conditions. It is impossible to feel depressed and negative while dancing.

movement as symbol

Movements have symbolic significance; take for instance the sweeping-out exercise mentioned on page 54: the sweeping movement enables you to visualize more strongly what you are trying to achieve.

However, movement has additional significance, because dancing rhythms raise power. Essentially, it is etheric energy, as discussed in the section on your aura. This energy, when it is strong, is easy to sense. It often spills out in ordinary life, such as at a football match or teenage disco – the atmosphere is electric! When this energy is directed and shaped, it is visible to those sensitive, and can be seen as a blue or gold cone or shower. You do not have to be able to see it clearly in order to direct it, however; the power of visualization and your will can do the trick.

Dancing will also have the effect of making you aware of your own body and its power, and so your connection with the Earth will be enhanced. An additional bonus is that dancing, because it is physical exercise, enables your body to release its own morphine equivalent as endorphins. Dancing is an excellent precursor to any type of ritual, however simple. Dance in a way that is pleasurable to you. Increase your heartbeat and respiration, but do not over-tire yourself! You need your energies for more cleansing.

dance to cleanse

1 If you feel an area needs a thorough cleansing and the idea of 'dancing it clean' appeals to you, play some music that you like, to get you in the mood. Dance very gently anti-clockwise (or clockwise in the Southern Hemisphere, since the movement should be opposite to the movement of the Sun); this is to 'undo' the negative energy.

2 Imagine you are unravelling a ball of wool. Imagine it stretching out, weakening and dispersing. When you feel this is complete, affirm that you have finished, stop, and touch the ground, to earth yourself.

3 Now begin to dance clockwise (anti-clockwise in the Southern Hemisphere). Put as much energy and joy into this as you wish, whirling, jumping, skipping and pirouetting. Imagine that you are raising a cone of power – shape it with your hands. Sing a chant, if that feels right.

4 When your cone is ready, send it off to do its work. Visualize it as a gold or white whirlwind, swirling through the area you wish to cleanse, driving out the negative stuff. Imagine it in every corner, and when you have finished, send it off to some deserted spot where anything unpleasant can be returned to the Earth and transformed.

5 When you have finished, bring yourself firmly back to earth by patting your body, touching your palms to the floor, and by eating and drinking something. Affirm that your chakras are closed, even if you did not intentionally open them. This exercise can leave you a bit drained at first, but with practice you will find it uplifting and reinvigorating.

PROTECTION TECHNIQUES

The cleansing and strengthening exercises given in the preceding chapters will afford you considerable protection and are a necessary preparation for strong defences. Doing them will help you build up your powers of visualization. Being able to visualize is essential and it is your strongest tool in psychic protection. Once something is real in your imagination, it is only a short step to making it real in the outside world.

In the following pages you will be asked repeatedly to 'visualize' or 'imagine' certain things. Many people worry that they cannot 'visualize' – they just do not 'see' things in their mind's eye – and believe that because of this they will not be able to achieve anything spiritual. However, this is not the case, and there is a way for everyone to create mental impressions. The problem really lies with the word 'visualize' since it gives the idea that all has to be visual. But it doesn't!

For those whose minds work visually, seeing things in pictures is relatively easy. But there are people who are more attuned to sound and others who are more attuned to feelings. Be aware of your own approach and adapt accordingly. For instance, if you are asked to 'imagine' a magic circle around you, it might suit you best to imagine hearing the circle humming like a power-circuit; or you might sense its 'atmosphere' or even smell or taste it. Strongly affirming that something is the case and believing it is also effective. It is also good to use props, such as pictures or symbols. Feel free to find what works for you.

visualization-applied imagination

Visualization is really applied imagination using the power of the mind, and imagination is the most powerful force in our lives. Everything you see and use, apart from what is actually living and growing on the Earth, existed in someone's imagination first of all. Your car existed in the mind of the designer, your house was born from an architect's imagination.

We are apt to be dismissive of this amazing force, saying, 'It's just imagination' as if imagination is less than 'reality'. However, in a battle between will and imagination, the latter always wins. For instance, if a plank half a metre (1½ ft) wide was placed on the floor you would walk along it with no problem. Place this plank across a deep ravine, and however sturdy the plank, most people would find that walk daunting. Willpower would not stop your palms sweating and your pulse racing. However, if you could imagine that plank was simply placed across the room, you would walk over it with no trouble at all!

how it works

There are two important pathways with respect to how imagination works. Firstly, imagination changes the mind and the mind in turn changes reality. It is easy to see this working: if you believe that people like you, and approach them in a friendly, open fashion as if they like you. Faced with that kind of behaviour, most people inevitably respond warmly, and so your belief is validated.

In the second place, imagination also works on the subtle planes (the astral plane). This means that imagination has an effect on a spiritual level, and this can and does translate to the physical. Sometimes the effect may not be obvious and sometimes it takes a while. At other times it is very evident to anyone with any sensitivity, such as when a depressed person creates a 'bad' atmosphere.

exercise your imagination

You can hone your imagination with a simple exercise. Place a favourite mug on the table in front of you. Now put the mug out of sight and imagine it is there. If you are not very visual you might imagine you can touch it or smell the coffee it contains. Concentrate for as long as you can. You are creating an image of that mug on the astral plane and when you stop concentrating, the 'astral' mug will gradually fade. However, anything that you imagine regularly, such as a protective magic circle, will have a permanent astral reality.

A simple exercise for imagination in a peaceful moment can greatly enhance your imaginative powers.

The mug exercise helps you develop astral 'muscle', although it achieves nothing useful in itself. However, you can get into the habit of powering-up your imagination in a way that is fun and useful. As you settle to sleep, imagine something that you want coming to pass in your life. Flesh it out in detail, live it and enjoy it, and drift off to sleep with it 'real' in your mind. Do this, night after night, with the same image. In due course you will find that it manifests for you.

your bubble of protection

We are all affected by auras in the natural world, so harness their force to work for you.

These are probably the most important pages in the book! Forming your bubble of protection is arguably the most significant step towards psychic defence. Once you have mastered it you can rely on being safe and secure, having created a strong astral sheath around yourself.

creating your bubble

When planning to perform this exercise for the first time, take a cleansing bath (see page 52). Cleanse your aura and follow this by cleansing the room where you are going to practise by sweeping and taking round the four elements (see pages 54–55). You may also use a bell, Tibetan singing bowl, music, incense or essential oils to create an uplifting environment (see pages 56–59).

1 Sit on a chair or lie down on your bed and relax (see pages 36–37). Be aware of your inner aura (your etheric) surrounding you and concentrate on its presence. Think of it as a skin or membrane around you, like a balloon. Imagine it contracting and expanding as you breathe in and out. Do this until you feel in control of this process.

2 Now, as you breathe out, imagine your auric sheath expanding, but do not contract it as you breathe in – make it expand, again like a balloon, until it forms a shining oval of white light surrounding you, about 70 cm (2 ft) from your body.

3 Repeat over and over again, 'I am safe, I am protected.' You may say this aloud if you wish. As you do so, imagine your protective bubble growing brighter and its skin is growing tougher. Imagine anything potentially harmful or hurtful bouncing off it and returning from whence it came.

4 When, and only when, you feel confident that this is established, affirm that your protective bubble is a magnet for anything positive and that benevolent, loving forces may enter through it, to bless you. Be careful that you progress to this only when you have strongly established your bubble as protection.

5 Affirm aloud if necessary, that whenever you need protection, your protective bubble will automatically appear. Repeat firmly to yourself, 'Whenever I need protection, it is there.' When you are ready, allow your bubble to shrink back, so it takes on the contours of your body once more, and let it decrease until it returns to the normal size of your etheric. Affirm that you are back to the here-and-now by eating and drinking something, patting your body and placing your feet to the floor.

6 Repeat this daily, for a month. It only takes about ten minutes. After that, reinforce it every few days, decreasing eventually to once a month. If you feel threatened, step up your practice sessions. Once you are used to doing this, you will be able to form your bubble instantly – when you are out and about or at work or wherever you need it. It will add greatly to your feelings of confidence and comfort.

the four elements

The ancients believed that everything was composed of the four elements Earth, Fire, Air and Water in different proportions, and with regard to energies, this still holds good. The four elements are fundamental vibrations or states of being that have reality on the physical level and also symbolic significance in the subtle realms. They cover the entire spectrum of the manifest world and are very important in psychic protection exercises.

associations and meanings

The descriptions of the four elements with their meanings and associations will help you bring the element more strongly into being when you need its attributes. By ancient systems of 'correspondences' each element is associated with symbols, substances, plants and crystals. However, nothing is engraved in tablets of stone, so if something feels right to you, go with it.

The qualities of these elements can be invoked and focused by using symbols and substances associated with them when you are doing exercises, and their qualities may be combined.

EARTH

SYMBOLS:	salt, stones, earth, pentagram (five-point star)
CRYSTALS:	green agate, jet, peridot, brown jasper
HERBS:	patchouli, honeysuckle, primrose, magnolia
COLOURS:	brown, black, dark green, some yellows and oranges

The element Earth relates to substances in the solid state. It is grounding, protective, nurturing, practical and stabilizing. Rituals to do with possessions, real estate, security, physical wellbeing and the bodily senses are all Earth matters. Money is also, but many occultists relate it to Air and computers.

WATER

SYMBOLS:	water in bowl, chalice, cauldron
CRYSTALS:	moonstone, amethyst, sapphire, chalcedony
HERBS:	lily, eucalyptus, hemp, jasmine
COLOURS:	purple, mid-greens, turquoise

This element relates to the liquid states and to feelings, memories, empathy, healing and cleansing. Rituals to do with calming, clearing emotions and feelings held, supported and understood are Water subjects, as are family, ancestors and community.

AIR

SYMBOLS:	joss stick, incense, wind-chimes
CRYSTALS:	aventurine, mottled jasper, blue-lace agate, citrine
HERBS:	lavender, lemongrass, mace, pine
COLOURS:	light blues, some yellows and oranges

Relating to gases, this element is also involved with communications, thoughts, intellectual matters, logic and movement. Rituals to do with clear thought, detachment, freedom and understanding are Air subjects, as are some money matters.

FIRE

SYMBOLS:	candle, sparkler
CRYSTALS:	amber, carnelian, sunstone, topaz
HERBS:	clove, orange, sunflower, coriander
COLOURS:	reds and oranges

The element Fire relates to substances that are volatile, vibrant and changing from one state to another. It is connected to energy, inspiration, creativity and courage. Rituals to do with changing, energizing, inspiring and empowering are Fire matters.

finding your dominant element

The elements are linked with human personality and each of us has one or two elements dominant within us. Recognizing which elements are strong and weak within you can help in becoming balanced and powerful. Moods can also be identified with the elements – for example, 'I'm all fired-up' or 'I'm all watery and emotional today'.

astrological clues

Another good indication of your dominant element can be your astrological sign. The Earth signs are Taurus, Virgo and Capricorn; the Water signs are Cancer, Scorpio and Pisces; the Air signs are Gemini, Libra and Aquarius; and the Fire signs are Aries, Leo and Sagittarius. However, your astrological sign is only your Sun sign and is only one aspect of your astrological make-up. If you have a chart drawn up for your date and time of birth, it may be that other elements are emphasized. You need to be open-minded when deciding which is your strongest element. Study the following descriptions and decide which one comes closest to you.

Earth

You are generally practical, with plenty of common sense. Aware of your body and its needs, you can be sensuous and self-indulgent. In general you cope well with schedules, organization and finances. Of all the elements you perhaps need protection the least frequently, because you are not easily fazed. Sometimes it is hard for you to see beyond the here-and-now and so you may feel in need of protection when faced with the volatile, the imagined and the changeable. You can be quite literal when dealing with spiritual matters, and may need Fire, in particular, to balance and encourage you.

Water

You tend to be emotional, sympathetic and to value close ties with others. Understanding others' needs, you can be very supportive, but you can also be over-sensitive and liable to take things personally. You are a romantic dreamer, gentle and caring, and while you may be very protective to others, you need help looking after yourself. The impartial and logical may seem like unkindness to you, and you may need Air, in particular, to give you some lightness and detachment, and guard you from upset.

Air

You tend to be chatty and communicative or wrapped up in your own thoughts. Generally you prefer everyone to be clear with you, to say what they think and sort things out, and you like using your mind and finding answers to problems. You can be very bright, witty and clear-thinking, but you may also be too detached, especially from your own feelings. This can lead to anxieties and nervousness. Emotions may seem like a quagmire to you, and you may need the gentle guidance of a little Water to help you to come to terms with the reality of your feelings and those of others, and to calm you down.

Fire

You are dynamic and forceful, generally appearing quite confident. You are an ideas person and to you the world is something of a playground. Often you are willing to trust your inner visions, but you can be less keen on the grim old realities of life such as the mortgage and daily routine. Your pride may be easily hurt, or you may feel crushed by too much of the mundane. The element Earth can help you to be more practical and protect you from falling foul of life's practicalities, enabling you to be stable and effectual.

elements in a magic circle

Your magic circle, guarded by the four elements — Air, Fire, Water and Earth — is a powerful protection.

Occultists perform their rituals within a magic circle made of 'mind stuff' that forms a strong barrier on the astral plane. While practitioners often use their magic circle to contain the power they raise, it is also a potent means of protection. 'Throwing a magic circle' around yourself or around a person or place will give them considerable psychic safety.

creating a magic circle

Your protective bubble, from a previous section, is a simplified magic circle. Make your bubble as wide as you like and then 'draw' round the circumference with your forefinger, a piece of quartz crystal or a smooth stick. Imagine that light is issuing from your finger or implement.

You can 'cast' the magic circle without doing the bubble exercise first. Often a circular rug helps to imagine this. Affirm that this magic circle is an impenetrable protection and reinforce this with as much visualization and imagination as you can. Your magic circle should be drawn 'sunwise' – clockwise in the Northern Hemisphere, anti-clockwise in the Southern Hemisphere.

elemental guardians

Now empower your magic circle with the elements in this order. Place a stone or similar (for Earth) in the north of your circle, a joss stick in the east (for Air), a candle in the south (for Fire) and a chalice of water in the west. (In the Southern Hemisphere, Fire should be in the north and Earth in the south.) These elemental powers are mighty guardians that will keep you safe. Ask for their special qualities as you place their symbols in the quarters, and imagine them entering your magic circle.

Use your magic circle for protection when meditating, opening your chakras, performing any spiritual exercise, or when sleeping, especially in a strange bed or when travelling. If you need to come in and out, open a 'doorway' with your finger and close it when you return. When you have finished with your magic circle, thank the elements in turn, starting with east/Air, and consciously reabsorb its energies.

If you feel you need a boost of a particular element, invoke it within your magic circle, using an object to represent the added element. Facing the appropriate direction, ask the object to empower you. As you do so, imagine the qualities that you want coming towards you. Ask for things aloud if you wish and give thanks afterwards.

Anything you use for the exercise – water or soil – should be placed outside on the Earth after use. As you become used to performing this sort of exercise, or when you have absorbed more associations described later in the book, you may want to extend your ritual by invoking certain deities, using symbols or essential oils, crystals and anything else that appeals.

use the power of nature

Don't forget the elements can be brought close for strengthening in daily life. Need Air? Walk in the wind, fly a kite. Need Earth? Do the gardening, repot houseplants. Need Fire? Light a bonfire or fireplace. Need Water? Go swimming, visit a stream or lake. Enjoy the elements and draw close to the powers of nature.

Bring the elements into your living space, as required, in any way that appeals to you.

the power of symbols

Symbols are an important part of your psychic arsenal. A meaningful symbol is much more than a glyph – it has resonance deep within you and can change your consciousness. Many symbols carry with them a train of associations that have an immediate effect on most people.

If you follow a spiritual path or religion, then the symbols connected with that path will be important to you. Objects and figures can have potent meaning (for example, a statue of the meditating Buddha). A symbol can also be totally personal, such as a ring that belonged to your mother or the teddy-bear you had as a child.

major symbols and their meanings

	SYMBOL	MEANING
	Cross	To Christians this is a symbol of Christ's sacrifice and redemption, but the older, Celtic equal-armed cross symbolizes the four elements, and when placed within a magic circle, represents the ritual magic circle described earlier.
	Five-pointed star	A favourite among modern nature-worshippers, it represents the four elements plus ether and the Goddess (with one apex pointing upwards, it echoes the female body). Also the shape reflects the pattern of the orbit of Venus.
	Ankh	The looped cross dates from ancient Egypt and is a symbol of life.
	Circle	Completion, infinity.
	Square	Protection, solidity.
	Triangle	Creativity (as in Mother, Father, Child). Also symbolizes the Trinity and the womb.

consecrating your symbol

The next section will help you discover your own special symbol if you are uncertain what it might be. It is a good idea to obtain your symbol as a figure, item of jewellery or similar and to 'consecrate' it (make it sacred) within your magic circle. This will imbue your symbol with unseen powers, as well as giving you confidence.

1 Using a small box or coffee-table, set up a simple altar in the north of your magic circle (south in the Southern Hemisphere). The altar is best in the mysterious, dark quarter, as what you are doing is an inward exercise. Place your stone on the altar and, as you are doing a ritual, two white candles as well. (Choose a red candle for the Fire quarter of your magic circle, to differentiate.) A figure of your favourite deity may go there too, along with the symbol you are consecrating. Some wine/juice and a little cake complete the picture.

2 Create your magic circle and hold your symbol, affirming it is special. Touch it to the stone, saying, 'Be blessed by Earth', then pass it through the incense smoke, saying, 'Be blessed by Air', next pass close to the Fire-quarter candle flame, saying, 'Be blessed by Fire' and finally anoint with or pass close to water, saying, 'Be blessed by Water'. As you do each of these things, imagine the qualities of the element entering your object.

3 Face your altar again and affirm that strong, pure energies are entering your symbol. Give thanks and celebrate by eating and drinking. Dismantle your magic circle when ready and dispose of left-overs by returning them to the Earth. Carry your symbol with you, sleep with it close and have it by you when meditating or performing any psychic exercise.

finding your power symbol

If you do not have a power symbol and nothing feels quite appropriate, try this meditation to help you discover it. Your subconscious holds its own wisdom and will likely be sheltering a symbol, or symbols, that mean power to you. To discover it you need to enter your own inner sacred space.

symbol meditation

Before you begin, reread 'Relaxation' on pages 36–37. Allow yourself to feel truly peaceful and tranquil. Play gentle music, without lyrics, if you like.

1 Affirm that you are safe (surround yourself with your bubble if you wish) and that you come in peace and love. Imagine yourself standing on an open plain. Around you dusk is falling and the sky is powdered with stars. The air is warm and a gentle breeze is blowing. Ahead is a majestic temple, silhouetted against the still-glowing sky.

2 Walk towards this temple. As you draw closer you realize how imposing it is. In the dim light you can make out wonderful statues lining your path. You hear the tinkle of wind-chimes and a faint scent of incense is reaching you. Slowly and steadily you approach.

3 The doorway is slightly open and through it you see a golden glow. Wonderful carvings surround this door. You pause. From within you hear the sound of chanting and the aroma of incense is stronger. You tap gently on the door. It swings inwards, smoothly and easily, as if inviting you to enter.

4 Enter the temple and find it lit by hundreds of candles. From deeper within the building the chanting intensifies, although it is still soft and subtle. The scent of incense is sweet and strong, and the smoke issues from ornate censers, spiralling in the golden light of the candles. Ahead is a large altar on which stand two enormous golden candlesticks, holding thick candles whose flames dance and glitter. Between the candlesticks is a wooden casket with two small doors. In front of these doors lies a golden key. You begin to walk towards the casket.

5 You are filled with excitement, for you know that the casket holds something special for you. When you arrive at the altar, you bow for a moment, giving thanks, then take the key and unlock the casket. Take your time about this.

6 Within the casket is your special, protective symbol. Take it, hold it to your chest. Bow again and give thanks, then walk back towards the door and out into the warm, fragrant evening. Hold your symbol to you beneath the vault of stars. Walk steadily until you arrive back into the here-and-now.

7 Sit up slowly, pat yourself and place your feet to the floor. Eat and drink something. Make a note of all you experienced.

8 In the everyday world, try to obtain your symbol in a form you can wear or carry. If this is impossible, then draw or find a picture of your symbol. If you are unsure about anything, repeat this meditation until you are certain. It may be that you have more than one symbol or other realizations may strike you as part of your inward journey.

Regular meditation can help you to unlock the doors to your own inner power.

deities

If you are committed to a particular faith, you will already have an idea about deity but, whatever your beliefs, you can still use specific deities since you are invoking their energies, in love, respect and peace, not making a theological statement. You may think of individual deities as differing manifestations of the One deity, or your concept may be that these are separate forces. Either way, they may be called upon for psychic protection.

Christian saints often carry the characteristics of older gods and goddesses – for instance, St Bridget has much in common with the Celtic goddess Bride. Angels, spirit guides and the like all come in this same category in respect of psychic protection – they are spiritual forces that will come when you call and lend you their guardianship.

your own deity

Having your own special deity will bring a great deal of comfort, since deity is a humanized manifestation of cosmic power. If you are not sure about a god or goddess for you, then you may use the visualization exercise on pages 76–77 to discover one. Change the script so the casket becomes a curtained shrine. When you reach this, the drapery moves aside to reveal your own deity, who may have words or a gift for you. If this happens, give thanks and honour that deity.

Try to obtain a figurine or picture of your goddess or god and place this somewhere safe in your home. Every so often, light a joss stick or place flowers before the figure, to show awareness and respect. In this way you are inviting this power to manifest in your life.

call on your deity for protection

Place the figure on your altar when you are performing protection rituals within your magic circle. Research and use symbols, plants and objects associated with your god or goddess to invoke their presence more fully. Carry or wear a representation of your deity, such as a medal or crystal. Do anything that feels right to bring you closer to your deity, and imagine your deity is with you when you need him or her.

It may also be a good idea to honour deities that you consider to be negative – warlike Mars, or Eris goddess of strife. These forces are real, and they have a purpose. Mars can be a real help if you need courage, and if a fight is inevitable, ask Mars that the conflict be fair and the outcome clear. And if a course you have chosen will obviously lead to strife, then honour Eris, asking her to enable all to air their views and to get these feelings out in the open. It is also good to honour such forces if you know they are within you, so you may express them with awareness and in balance, neither being possessed by them nor trying to repress them.

All the goddesses and gods have valuable characteristics and their own domain. Honouring them brings smooth transitions in life. This is something the ancients knew very well, and has nothing to do with being judgmental or about 'right' or 'wrong'. These are the forces of nature and it is about having balance in all things. This balance is the basis of power.

a selection of deities

Below are six gods and goddesses, along with some of their associations, chosen to cover a variety of themes that may be useful to you. Please read and research further if you want to find a deity that feels really close to you. Consider significant times in your life to date. Has there been a saint, mythical figure or deity that has always drawn you or seemed to pop up – in street names, literature or any other way. Then maybe that power is trying to get closer to you. Keep an open mind.

Venus is one of the most beloved of goddesses, whose power can help you to protect a relationship.

Isis

This Egyptian goddess is a very complete form of feminine deity. She is a lover, wife, mother, widow, patroness of creativity, presiding over cornfield, ocean and the courts of kings. The pharaoh ruled by her authority. She is wonderful for feminine power, to retain dignity, to connect to one's womanhood, and to cope with multi-tasking.

Associations: Ankh, throne, ruby, sapphire, olive, narcissus, owl, lion, myrrh, cedar

Thoth

Egyptian god of wisdom, Thoth is just and benevolent, precise and detached. He was shown with the head of an ibis, and is a healer and magical partner to Isis. Thoth is a potent god if you need to separate from raw emotions, to retain a wide perspective and to think clearly.

Associations: Writing materials, fire opal, almond, scrolls

Venus

She is well known as the love-goddess, and while she may bring danger in the shape of wild passion, she is also caring towards those who love and can help you to protect a viable relationship. Venus is beautiful and sensuous, and can help you to honour and pleasure your body.
Associations: Adornments, mirrors, emerald, turquoise, swan, rose, myrtle

Jupiter

He is the Roman king of the gods, larger-than-life, bringing good fortune, laughter, riches and power. He is a wonderful ally if you need to be optimistic, positive and to project your personality so you get your own way. He is also mightily protective, especially of those who are brave and do their best.
Associations: Wheel of fortune, lightning, amethyst, eagle, clove, sage

Kwan Yin

She is a Buddhist goddess and the most powerful figure in the Chinese pantheon. She is a great lover of humanity and brings peace and understanding. Hers is a gentle, protective but infinitely wise presence and she will guard you while meditating, or when you are trying to do good to others.
Associations: Children, lotus, lily, lion, jade

Cernunnos

He is the Celtic horned god, protector of the wild creatures deep in the forest. He is also god of the hunter, and the patron of the cycle of life, in which hunter and prey are each a part. He brings the indescribable peace and sense of rightness that comes upon you when close to nature, and can protect you from anyone who would do violence to natural law.
Associations: Horns, stone, moss agate, all horned animals especially the stag, patchouli

Kwan Yin's gifts of peace and comfort are unrivalled. She is a great benefactress to humanity.

power animals

In tribal cultures, shamans or magical priests often have power animals that protect and empower them during spirit flights. It is the animal spirit that is present, although individual animals do often come as representatives. A power animal brings with it a very special and potent energy of the natural world, and your special animal (or animals) can be a mighty ally in confronting life.

meeting your power animal

1 If you are not sure about your power animal, adapt the visualization method described on pages 76–77 to meet your animal. Instead of the temple, find yourself approaching a forest. Enter it and be aware of the ancient trees with their tangle of branches and roots underfoot.

2 Push your way through the undergrowth until you emerge into a clearing, which has a huge tree with low-hanging branches. There is also a cave and a lake, lying deep and serene.

3 Hear the rustle of wild things in the forest and the cries of birds. Smell the earth and the herbal tang of the greenery. Wait peacefully until your animal comes to you. Speak to your animal, travel with your animal and follow where it leads.

4 When this is completed, come back to where you started, say 'thank you' and take respectful leave, walking back out of the forest and into the here-and-now. Remember to ground yourself, as explained in 'Closing down your chakras' on page 49.

5 Once discovered, you can keep your power-animal effigy near you during exercises or wear it as jewellery when you feel you need protection. Carry a part of an animal that has been obtained naturally, say an owl feather you have found on the ground. Call on your animal to go with you into difficult situations. Having Bear padding beside you or Eagle perched on your shoulder will give you strength and confidence.

You may already have chosen an animal that represents qualities that you want. Possibly you are aware of needing an animal quality, as in 'I could do with the strength of an ox!' or 'the cunning of a fox'. Sometimes, however, we can be surprised at the animal we need — it is much easier to get excited about Lion or Eagle than about Mouse or Frog!

A power animal is not the same as a totem. For instance, your family may always have loved Siamese cats or Labradors, and these animals are a sign of kinship. It may be that this animal is your power animal, but do not assume this without deep thought. Is this animal energy truly what you need? If not, search elsewhere.

ANIMAL	SYMBOLISM AND MEANING
Owl	Wisdom
Stag	Pride, independence
Bear	Power, instinct
Fox	Cunning, diplomacy
Hawk	Nobility, memory
Dog	Guidance, protection
Cat	Guardianship, aloofness, sensuality
Frog	Sensitivity, hidden beauty
Raven	Initiation, protection
Swan	Love, beauty
Wolf	Intuition, path-finding, learning, teaching

ANIMAL	SYMBOLISM AND MEANING
Snake	Healing, transformation
Eagle	Courage, far-sightedness
Sow	Nourishment, new meanings
Bull	Potency, wealth
Ram	Achievement, breakthrough
Hare	Intuition, rebirth
Salmon	Wisdom, knowledge
Bee	Industry, organization
Otter	Joy, play
Horse	Travel, the power within the land

crystals

Crystals carry many different energy-signatures, so it is always worthwhile getting to know them.

Crystals are great friends when it comes to psychic protection. Formed millions of years ago, crystals bring with them the wisdom of the ages. Each one has a symmetrical atomic structure and although it appears tranquil, it is a powerhouse of unseen energies. Every crystal has its specific 'energy-signature', and almost any crystal can be some help towards psychic protection. Crystals have long been credited with therapeutic and spiritual effects and are also seen as channels of power or blessing. You may simply view them as a way to focus your mind and access your abilities. Whatever the case, there will be a special crystal, or crystals, for you.

choosing a crystal

A huge variety of crystals are readily available as cheap tumble-stones, but when choosing a crystal for psychic protection, formulate clearly within your mind how you want to feel. When choosing, decide which one generates that feeling for you. Be aware of bodily sensations and emotions aroused. Crystals often seem to 'call' you. Don't worry, you can't get it wrong, but some may be more right than others! Treat crystals with respect, for some have hard-to-handle energies, such as malachite and obsidian; and don't sleep with a crystal close to you unless you are very sure about it.

cleansing

Cleanse your crystal by holding it in a stream (or under running water). Alternately, leave it overnight on an amethyst cluster or simply visualize it bathed in a shower of white light. Store it carefully, wrapped in velvet and 'charge it up' with your own energies by holding it between your palms and sending loving life-force into it.

Use running water to help cleanse your crystals.

crystal protection

1 To programme your crystal to protect you, create your ritual magic circle (see pages 72–73) and sit in the middle facing your Earth quarter, with your crystal in front of you and a large white candle beside it.

2 Light the candle, and as the light spreads out, imagine a radiance coming from the crystal, forming a protective sphere around you. When you feel sure this is strongly in place, imagine it being reabsorbed by the crystal, snuff out your candle and give thanks to the crystal spirit.

3 Carry the crystal with you to feel safe, and when you need a protective boost, imagine the crystal is emitting its sphere. Always remember to reabsorb this, or you could find yourself sealed off against beneficial energies too!

CRYSTAL	MEANING
Bloodstone	Strengthens your wits, protects health, keeps you grounded and effectual.
Carnelian	Gives courage and vitality.
Chalcedony	Brings positive thoughts and faith in life.
Garnet	Brings power and energy.
Jade	Brings good judgement and attracts friends.
Red jasper	Helps you be honest with yourself and face conflict. It also brings attractiveness.
Jet	Repels evil and brings control.
Labradorite	Brings psychic protection and safety from the beliefs of others.
Lapis lazuli	Repels suffering and cruelty.
Malachite	Protects finances and makes you aware of danger but keep it away from your body if you feel 'peculiar'.
Onyx	Supportive and protects your secrets.
Snowflake obsidian	Absorbs negative energies and stops you fearing fear itself.

trees, plants and flowers

The subtle effects of plants are to be cherished. Allow yourself to become aware of them.

Members of the plant kingdom have their own characteristics and many can be added to your protection arsenal. We looked at the power of scent and incense in the section on cleansing. Anything that cleanses will also protect because it drives away harm and negativity. While smell easily changes consciousness, you do not have to smell plant materials in order to benefit from their protective qualities.

flower remedies

A more subtle use of plants is provided by Bach Flower Remedies. These use the subtle energies of the plant to treat psychological conditions that also give rise to physical symptoms. They are not the same as essential oils, which are simply concentrated plant materials. Bach Flower Remedies are preserved in brandy and can be taken internally: place two drops of a 'stock' remedy in a glass of spring water and sip at intervals.

small rituals

There are many reassuring little rituals you can do with plants and trees. These are all based on traditional associations.

- Place a little sprig of basil in each room of the house for protection.

- A bay tree near the house protects from sickness, a sprig hung indoors drives away poltergeists and carrying a bay leaf is all-round protection.

- An ordinary three-leaf clover is a protective amulet while a four-leaf one is very lucky in general.

- Carrying comfrey gives safety during travel, and a leaf in your suitcase will prevent it being stolen.

- Garlic is very strongly protective. Hung around the house it drives away evil and rubbed on to cooking pots it repels any negativity in the food.

- Rowan protects any home it grows near.

- Mint kept in the home will protect it.

- Carrying any piece of the oak is protective and lucky; and acorn aids creativity.

This can be repeated several times in a day. Rescue Remedy, which is a combination of Cherry Plum, Clematis, Rock Rose, Impatiens and Star of Bethlehem essences, is used to treat shock and can be placed directly on the tongue. The essences can be sprayed around an area, for similar effect.

REMEDY	HELPS TREAT
Rescue Remedy	Helps calm you down if you are in a state of shock or agitation.
Larch	Drives away depression and low self-esteem.
Crab Apple	Cleanses those who feel inwardly 'unclean'.
Holly	Diffuses strongly negative emotions such as anger, jealousy and bitterness.
Walnut	Very protective in times of change; protects against subtle attack. Can break ties with negative associations of all kinds.
Agrimony	Helps those who hide their true feelings and seek excitement including drugs to dull inner pain.
Centaury	Strengthens the timid, anxious and easily dominated.
Sweet Chestnut	Eases anguish and despair.
Star of Bethlehem	For fright and shock.
Rock Rose	To deal with terror and hysteria.
Mimulus	Helps any specific physical fear — heights, for example.
Cherry Plum	Calms fear of nervous breakdown.
Aspen	Calms vague apprehensions and dreads.
Red Chestnut	Keeps fears for others in perspective.
Gorse	Alleviates despair.

It can feel threatening when you have to share your personal space with strangers.

protection in the city

When in a crowded city or any place where there are lots of people, our subtle senses and auras are continually under assault. We all know that strangers can indeed be a physical threat, but instinctively we react against what is unseen – the thoughts and feelings of anyone unfamiliar. For this reason people on public transport avoid eye-contact. Being forced into such close proximity, people 'close down' by not looking. While this is a form of protection, it can also make you feel lonely and isolated.

In small towns it is considered quite acceptable to say 'Hello' to strangers walking dogs and to smile at people in the street. But this sort of behaviour is not common in cities. If you are used to life in a big city, you will intuitively have evolved ways of dealing with this. However, you may not be aware of the toll it is taking on you.

city behaviour

When on a train or bus or any other public place, cross your arms and legs. This is an old sign of protection. Turn your mind inwards and dwell on pleasant thoughts, happy memories, people you love and bright plans for the future. Remember your protective bubble and form this before going out. When it is properly in place, see it grow 'spikes' – not sharp spikes designed to cause injury, but little electric protuberances that will warn off anything harmful on any level.

Naturally, if you are in a crowded place, your auric space will be invaded, so affirm that your protective auric bubble bends inwards to accommodate this, remaining intact, and springs back out as soon as there is space. Please remember to reabsorb the energies of your 'bubble' as soon as you feel safe, otherwise there will be a barrier between you and others, even in regard to good things, like love and caring. When you get home after being exposed to lots of strangers, have a bath or shower and visualize and affirm that you are 'washing off' negative energies.

a magic circle for safety

For extra protection, make yourself a herbal sachet. If you are good at sewing, make it in the form of a magic circle or a square, since either of these shapes suggests balance and completeness. Otherwise, a circle of felt tied up as a bag with ribbon or string will do! The herbs should have a smell that pleases you, so that you can sniff it in order to change your mood. Choose blue felt for peace, green for healing and soothing brown for solidity and security or orange for cheering and heartening.

You could include lavender for peace, orange peel for a boost, rosemary for clear thought and mustard seed to give a psychic kick to anything nasty. Assemble all your materials within your protective magic circle and make your sachet while thinking positive thoughts – play music if it helps. Ask your deity to bless your sachet and carry it with you whenever you need to feel safe in a crowded place.

Making your own herbal sachet for safety is a comforting thought in a hectic world.

protection at work

A crystal placed on your desk will help you feel protected and can also help your body deal with computer radiation.

Everyone needs a safe and peaceful environment in order to do their best. So much of life is spent at work that it is a great shame to go through it feeling miserable. It is impossible to be creative in an atmosphere of strife.

creating a peaceful space

If you work in an office you will not have control over what happens around you, so 'programme' a crystal to give you a peaceful, protected space. Choose a crystal that you feel is suitable, in a shape that will be convenient. If you have space on your desk, it may be worth investing in a fairly large crystal ball. If you need to be more discreet, choose a small crystal or one you can wear. If your job involves moving around a lot, the latter will be the best choice. Programme your crystal within your magic circle (see pages 72–73), but reinforce the fact that the crystal will protect you in a work environment. Say these words: 'Crystal pure to you I pray, Whilst I'm at work keep harm at bay.'

As you say the words imagine a glow emanating from the crystal, surrounding you and repelling harm of any kind. Then imagine the glow being reabsorbed by the crystal. Do this several times until it comes easily. When you feel you need this protection in a work situation, say the words under your breath and let the crystal do its stuff. Always remember to say thanks and let the crystal reabsorb the sphere of light.

safe public speaking

You can use the same technique for public speaking or giving presentations at work. Here your crystal will be 'busier' for the glowing sphere it emanates needs to protect you, but also to attract smiles and applause. Take the time to imagine this when you are calm within your magic circle and holding your crystal. Touch it and look at it before you start to speak and affirm that your sphere is in place. Every so often, cleanse your crystal in a fresh stream or spring water – after all, it's working hard!

If you are unfortunate enough to work with an aggressive, unhearing, insensitive individual, your best bet is to get out. Nothing is worth that kind of strain and you have nothing to prove. However, if you really have to stay, then try this. You will need a black candle, black thread, white paper and a black pen. Make your magic circle as usual and light the black candle. Write the name of the person who is tormenting you on the paper with the pen, along with a description of their behaviour. Bind it into a scroll with the thread, saying: 'With this thread I bind you, No more harm to do.' Say this at least three times. When you have dismantled your magic circle, place the scroll in the freezer and leave it there as long as it needs to stay 'cool'.

A binding ritual can be effective when someone is pressurizing you, yet causes you no distress.

protecting relationships

Your relationship circle is a testimony to the value you place on your partnerships.

It would be very wrong and ultimately counterproductive to attempt to 'protect' a relationship where the other party wishes to be free. However, where you are both committed to nurturing your relationship, it is as well to work on the subtle planes as well as on the practical.

a relationship circle

You will need a sizeable notice-board that you should hang in your home for this exercise. On this board pin an embroidery hoop, which you should paint deep pink (or any colour that signifies love and warmth to you). Around the hoop pin as many pleasant mementos of your love as you can find. These could be cards you've sent each other, theatre tickets, photos and anything you like. You can decorate it with things you simply find pretty and romantic.

divisible by four

Divide your embroidery hoop into equal segments by stretching lengths of ribbon across its diameter. Select how many segments you need and what these should be devoted to, but if possible keep to four, eight or 12 as these numbers are divisible by four, and echo the four elements within the magic circle. In this way your relationship circle signifies completeness and balance. You could simply have Air (time spent discussing things, shared interests), Fire (fun and passion), Water (cuddles, affection, listening to each other's troubles), and Earth (sorting out money, doing housework).

Or you could plot your year on your circle, showing all the things you have done together, month by month, symbolically. Be inventive. It doesn't so much matter how you do this, as long as it looks balanced and gives you both pleasure. At important times or on special dates, such as your anniversary, light a candle near your notice-board, add something to it and celebrate in the way you choose.

breaking the ties that bind

You may need protection of a different kind, from someone with whom you once had a relationship but who, for some reason, will not leave your heart and/or life. It does not matter who is at fault – the object is to break the ties.

You will need a picture or other representation of your ex (their name written on a scrap of paper, for example) and similar for yourself, black thread, a piece of labradorite crystal and dried rose petals. Tie one end of the thread around the picture of your ex and the other round your picture. Say: 'I break the ties twixt me and thee, Apart and happy, so may it be.' Cut the thread in two and wrap the longest end round the picture of your ex, folding rose petals within it. Burn all in a heat-proof container and empty the ashes outside. Wrap your own picture up with rose petals and labradorite and place it somewhere safe, for as long as you need to. Repeat this as often as you like, cleansing the labradorite each time.

An effective ritual gets the message through to your subconscious loud and clear.

Please note, none of these exercises are designed to interfere with the free will and life path of another person – only to keep you safe and free.

protecting children and pets

Protecting a child or much-loved pet may be far more important to you than protecting yourself. There are several things you can do to make sure that your love goes with your loved ones, keeping them safe and secure.

cat protection

Bach Flower Remedies offer gentle yet powerful protective essences, especially when 'charged up'.

Cats are perhaps the hardest animals to protect, because they are so independent and come and go as they please. To protect your cat, obtain a small effigy of Bast, the Egyptian cat goddess. Place this on a small shelf and underneath it put a scrap of your cat's fur. Ask Bast to look after your cat. Heat a fragrance such as orange, cinnamon or frankincense in an oil-burner near her effigy every so often as an offering.

charging up Flower Remedies

You may anoint cats, dogs and children with a Bach Flower Remedy that you have 'charged up'. Walnut or Centaury are good choices. Place a few drops of the remedy in a little water in a glass, and, sitting within your magic circle, hold the glass between your palms. Imagine your child or pet surrounded by protection, happy, smiling and safe. Imagine these good feelings and good images going into the remedy. Afterwards, place a little on the forehead of your child or pet. (This should be suitable even for very tiny babies, but avoid the eyes.) In the case of uncooperative teenagers, dab some remedy on their clothes, when they aren't looking!

send in your power animal

If you are especially worried about your child, summon your power animal to go with him or her. Do your visualization to meet with your power animal, as described on pages 82–83. Since you want to meet an animal that will protect your child, do not be surprised if a creature different from your own power animal appears within the clearing and approaches you.

Ask if it comes in peace and love, and be sure you are happy with the answer. Explain to the animal that you wish it to look after your child and ask if it will accompany you. If it agrees, walk with it out of the forest clearing and into the everyday world. Take great care now to ground yourself, because you have brought the spirit animal with you and that could mean you feel 'spaced out'. Walk barefoot on grass and eat a meal.

Reinforce the presence of the animal by placing its pictures near your child, visualizing it, 'smelling', 'hearing' or 'feeling' it. Don't forget to thank and honour it. Do something to help the species in the everyday world as a sign of gratitude. When the task is complete, repeat your inward journey, taking your animal back into the forest clearing, and say goodbye with a final thank you.

Children instinctively carry their own symbol of protection – you can strengthen these.

guardian angels

Finally, small children are very close to the spirit world and their guardian angels are near by. Whatever your beliefs, you can pray to the angel, asking it to guide you to wise choices. Spirits often reside in much-loved toys too, so Teddy may be more important than you think!

The image of St Christopher has protected many people over many years while travelling.

protection while travelling

St Christopher, the patron saint of travellers, adorns medals that are often worn as a protection while travelling. Whatever your religion, they are a powerful symbol for protection and it is not the religious dogma that counts, but the intention and the love. If you wear a St Christopher medal, light a white candle and, holding your medal, ask the saint for protection. Imagine his benevolent presence carrying you through your journey. It is always good to give back, so donate a little to a life-saving charity as a 'thank you'.

safe driving

To make your car safe, cleanse it in the same way as your house (see pages 54–55). Bless it with the four elements, moving around the symbols of the elements within the space of the car's interior: ask for the blessing of Air for lightness, smoothness, freedom from hitches; Fire for strength and alertness; Water for comfort and peaceful journeys; and Earth for good solid protection and reliability.

Place within your car your protective symbol or a crystal of your choice. Take the elements around the outside of your car, affirming that your car is protected in all ways, from all directions. Form your protective symbol with your forefinger, at the front, the back and each of the sides, and also over the top and underneath (you will have to visualize/affirm this, if you can't reach!). It may be best not to put a protective bubble around the car, however, unless you are very sure of your skills, because you do not want to reduce your ability to perceive what is around you.

Making jewellery can be a very protective ritual and will calm and soothe you.

the comfort of home

When you are going on a long journey, especially one you are not sure about, take along the warmth and safety of home with this little exercise.

1 Obtain a length of cord and beads in a variety of colours that you can thread on this. You are going to make a simple bracelet, so choose beads and cord accordingly – an elasticated cord may be best. The best colour for the cord is brown or dark green.

2 Now think of all the things about home you value – the comfort of your room, your family, your books, music. For each of these things choose a bead. Red and pink beads may symbolize love and affection, blue for uplifting things like books, green for your garden. Thread each one on your cord, saying: 'I name this one for …, and I take it with me to protect and bless me.' When you have completed your bracelet, secure the beads with a knot and make it ready to go on your wrist. Hold it between your palms and say: 'My home comes with me to protect me, and soon I shall be back in my home, Blessed Be.'

DRAWING POSITIVE ENERGIES

When you are concentrating on protecting yourself, you are turning your attention towards negative forces – namely those you perceive as a threat. While it is certainly desirable to have strong defences, and it is true that there are harmful forces that may need to be dealt with, it is all too easy to forget the positive approach.

When your life contains joy, laughter, love and productive things to do, it is much harder for anything nasty to gain a foothold. In fact there are some people who will probably never need psychic protection, because they are so fundamentally positive that anything potentially harmful is powerless against them.

It is very easy to say 'Think positive!', but not nearly so easy to do! Sadly, there is a type of sanctimonious New Age elitism that sometimes judges people for being 'negative' or 'unspiritual'. This is unfair, for no one can ever know what another person has had to deal with; furthermore repressing the negative can be very unsound psychological practice. Nonetheless, it is wise to learn to be as positive as you can, since it makes life more enjoyable, and a cheerful outlook can radically change your life, enabling you to discover new sides to yourself and new talents.

In this chapter we shall look at making your approach more positive, learning new habits and turning to new perspectives, as well as considering spirit beings and blessings. If you have been used to thinking in one way all your life, an alteration to another way will hardly be instantaneous. However, it is possible to make changes, to find greater joy and to fill your life with blessings.

positive thinking

Directing your thoughts positively can result in enhanced creativity and greater spiritual health.

Positive thinking is not about pretending things are great when they manifestly are not; it is about seeing as much good around you as possible. It is not about repressing your feelings of sadness, loss, anger and similar, but it involves fully experiencing such feelings, maybe choosing to act upon them, but then letting them go and allowing better things to flow towards you.

here are some approaches for you to try

- 'The devil makes work for idle hands!' The 'devil' of course, is negativity. Keep busy. If you do not have a job, do voluntary work, clean your house, go for walks. If you are feeling low this will feel very much against the grain at first, but try it a little at a time, building up as your energy and inclination grow.

- Avoid depressing headlines – seek out publications like *Positive News*.

- Regularly smile at yourself in the mirror, and give yourself praise!

- At the end of each day write down three good things that have happened, that you have seen or know about.

- Also write down three things you have achieved, that have made something or someone better. This includes sitting and stroking your cat or doing some washing, as well as pulling off a marvellous deal at work or writing a chapter.

- At the end of each day read something uplifting and cheering, such as poetry or a novel with a happy ending.

- Keep a compliments diary, in which you record all the nice things others say about you, however trivial they might seem.

- Count your blessings – write these down too. There are many things in life that are blessings, that we simply take for granted. For instance, food on the table, safety from physical attack, running water – the list is almost endless.

- Phone your friends and family and tell them some good news!

- Have a laugh, especially with friends.

- Have sex – it's truly life-affirming.

- Choose two or three reasonable positive affirmations that you can say to yourself with conviction. For instance, it may be useless to say over and over again 'I am happy, I am happy!' when you are miserable. What you could say is 'I am finding things to cheer me up!'

- Do a kind deed, such as helping an old person (but not if one of the reasons you feel negative is because you are always having to do things for other people).

- Have a small treat every day (a glass of wine, bar of chocolate, sit in sunshine) and a big one each week (have a massage or a night out with friends).

- If something bad happens to you, such as losing your job, list all the benefits that could come your way through this in the short-term and long-term. For example: 'Thank goodness I don't have to get up so early!' to 'Maybe I can now retrain for the career I want.'

hypnotherapy

Sometimes it can be hard to change your outlook without help. Seeking help is a sign of strength, not weakness – it takes courage to admit that something is wrong and good sense to do something about it.

subconscious activity

A negative outlook on life often arises at a subconscious level, and while the exercises given in the previous section will go some way towards altering this, results may be gained more swiftly by acting directly on the subconscious. This can be achieved through hypnotherapy.

Although many stage acts show hypnosis as something rather alarming, therapeutic hypnotherapy is nothing like the theatrical variety. It can be described as a process of 'verbal massage'. Most therapists induce a relaxed state simply by talking to the patient who is lying down, warm and comfortable. In my practice I also play soft music and tape-record everything I say, so that the patient has a cassette to take home to play daily, so intensifying the process.

Once you are relaxed, your subconscious mind is 'open' and will soak up positive affirmations. It will be similar to that lovely drowsy, drifty stage between waking and sleeping. This isn't a weird trance that you have never experienced before, but a normal state of mind, the only difference being that in this case the mental state is being put to good use. The effects of this are often quite powerful, depending on how good a subject you are, but given time, results can be obtained with almost anyone.

positive suggestions

As you lie back, relaxing, the therapist will embark upon positive suggestions, telling you that you are becoming more confident, stronger, happier or possibly asking you to visualize yourself being successful at a task, facing a situation serenely or similar. The choice of 'script' will depend on the condition for which you are seeking help. Affirmations that

are not too far away from your usual outlook generally are most effective. For instance, if you have been very anxious and are suffering from panic attacks, to be told during your first hypnotherapy session that you are totally relaxed, confident and fearless may be so counter to your experiences that you are brought out of the hypnotic state. Often it is better to 'programme' a small improvement, such as 'becoming calmer, day by day', and to build on this.

Hypnotherapy is a pleasant relaxing experience and can have powerful effects on your spiritual wellbeing.

positive injections

If you feel you need an injection of positivity to turn you around, hypnotherapy can be a very powerful tool. Therapists can be found on the web, at local holistic healing centres or in the local press. Always ensure that your therapist is qualified and belongs to a professional body. Personal recommendation is often best. Hypnotherapy can improve your state of mind, making you able to resist negativity and to make the most of your life.

By far the best bet is to find a good therapist; however, you can hypnotize yourself, simply by relaxing (see page 102). Decide beforehand on some simple affirmations that you are going to repeat to yourself when you are relaxed, or record your voice and play it back, telling yourself you are optimistic, positive or whatever you want to be. Keep this within reasonable bounds and build on your achievements. Wake yourself up by affirming strongly that you are awake, alert and back to normal.

angels

Angels are spirit messengers, and while images of angels come to us from Christian, Islamic, Judaic and Zoroastrian traditions, they have relevance for all humans. Beings from a higher realm, bringing tidings of hope, joy, protection and love, they can be prayed to or invoked with great confidence.

Some people believe that angels were humans who have evolved to a higher state, while others hold that they are different entities entirely. Angels make themselves known to us in human form, so that we may relate to them. In art angels are often depicted wearing long robes and having wonderful wings. This conveys their spirituality and enables human beings to have faith that one day, they too will be able to soar above the confines of the petty and find a true home for the soul.

angel visits

These beings often visit us when we are at our most desperate and fearful, appearing surrounded by light, bringing sweet music or wonderful scent with them. Less dramatically, you may know that an angel has visited you by finding a feather near your bed or elsewhere in the house.

We all have a guardian angel, who may whisper to us in times of danger, causing us to change our plans; later we find out that this has saved us from injury or even saved our lives. Your guardian angel will speak to you if you ask for guidance from a pure motive. Light a white candle and simply pray in whatever way seems right. Pledge a helpful deed for someone else as a 'thank you'. This is not to 'pay' the angel or prove that you are unselfish, but to set up a flow between you and the Cosmos.

angel hierarchy

Archangels are a higher form of angel with more far-reaching powers. Medieval magicians used them in invocations and you can invoke them to empower you in certain situations, by asking for their presence and surrounding yourself with their symbols.

MICHAEL

CRYSTAL: Citrine or clear quartz
INCENSE OIL: Frankincense/orange
CANDLE COLOUR: Gold

The angel of light, Archangel Michael is a warrior who drives away darkness.
He wields a mighty sword and may carry scales, to weigh souls.

GABRIEL

CRYSTAL: Moonstone
INCENSE OIL: Jasmine
CANDLE COLOUR: Silver

Known as the 'Strength of God', Gabriel brings psychic power, wisdom, vision
and procreation. He is heard chiefly in dreams and linked to the Moon. Gabriel
is associated with wonderful messages and is often portrayed carrying a lily or
sceptre. He is the angel of the Annunciation – the messenger from God to the
Virgin Mary with news that she would bear His son.

RAPHAEL

CRYSTAL: Aquamarine or jade
INCENSE OIL: Pine
CANDLE COLOUR: Green

Healer of all life, Raphael is the guardian of the young and of travellers, often
linked with Mercury. He is shown with a staff, a fish and a wallet.

AURIEL

CRYSTAL: Carnelian
INCENSE OIL: Sandalwood
CANDLE COLOUR: Red

'Fire of God', Auriel is associated with storms and earthquakes, and is the
bringer of salvation, courage and wisdom, and may be linked with Mars.

spirit guides

The Native Americans lived in tune with nature and many spirit guides came to them there.

Many traditions have spirit guides. These are usually helpful people from the past and/or from other cultures who have progressed to a higher form in spirit, but who are willing to remain attached to the Earth plane to help humans evolve. Your spirit guide could be someone with whom you had a relationship in a past life or a being with whom you have an affinity. He or she may well be an aspect of your Higher Self that is not normally present in day-to-day consciousness.

sensible spirit guides

Spirit guides are teachers, while angels are messengers, but sometimes their roles seem to overlap. Your spirit guide/s will have specific personalities, sometimes humorous, always benevolent and supportive, and sensible! Any 'guide' who says you are a reincarnation of Cleopatra or Napoleon, or are destined to save the planet is probably a projection of your ego. Keep a sense of proportion your feet on the ground.

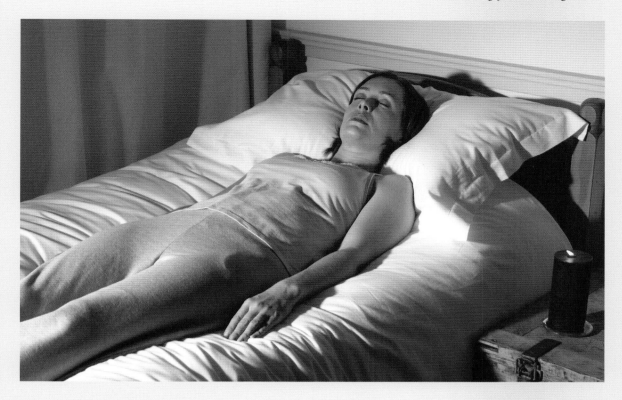

meeting your spirit guide

We probably have two guides – one male and one female – bringing their own 'energies' and gifts. To discover and meet your guides, try this visualization.

1 Relax deeply. Imagine that it is a lustrous night, with a full Moon. You are standing at the bottom of a hill, with the scent of grass and sweet earth around you. You look up towards the top of the hill and see a circle of standing stones, silhouetted in the moonlight. Two of the largest stones stand, large and imposing with a third placed across them, forming a gateway. Slowly you walk up the hill towards this entrance.

2 Walking between the stones, you slowly enter the circle. Here the moonlight glows and the mighty stones cast shadows of ebony. The air is soft and still and a gentle fragrance hangs in the night air. All is peaceful, and while you feel a thrill of expectancy and a sense of mystery, you feel safe and uplifted.

3 In front of you, to your right and to your left, two shadows emerge from the shadows and move inwards. Soon two wonderful beings – male and female – move into the centre of the circle. The moonlight bathes them and your spirit guides become visible. Look closely at them, at their clothes, faces and general demeanour. Speak to them, touch or embrace them, tell them you are glad to see them. Ask them who they are and listen with your 'mind's ear' to the answer, which may come to you in written words or pictures.

4 Spend as much time as you wish in conversation. When you are ready, take respectful leave, come back down the hill and into everyday awareness. Write down what you have experienced and repeat this exercise regularly, until you feel in contact with your guides in daily life.

blessing and healing

Blessing is a process of drawing positive and loving influences towards a person or thing. In fact, many of the protection exercises in the previous chapters also involve some 'blessing' because they include a summoning of purer energies. Issue blessings when you feel empowered by love.

offer yourself as a channel

The energy-signature of water can be changed by your intentions and can carry blessings.

When you bless, you are offering yourself as a channel for healing and grace. Signs of blessing are simply outward signals to the instinctual parts of yourself that this process is taking place. A yoga *mudra*, the cross and the pentagram are all symbols of blessing. Your power symbol, discovered on pages 74–77, is also a sign of blessing. Choose whatever feels most comfortable, meaningful and spiritual as your blessing-signature.

As a simple blessing for people and things, consecrated water may be best. Life depends on and is largely composed of water, and water has the power to absorb both feelings and intentions. Water molecules alter in response to subtle signals, so you may be sure that water you have truly blessed will have something special about it.

Place some spring water in a glass or earthenware vessel. Avoid plastic – it is too synthetic. Light a white candle and place your protective bubble around you. You may cast a full magic circle, if you wish, as explained on pages 72–73. Open your chakras and draw golden light into your crown chakra. Feel it gathering in your navel, ready to be transmitted down your arms. Or you may simply sit quietly, allowing yourself to be filled with love and peace.

Ask that you may be a channel for good. Hold your hands, palms downwards, over the bowl of spring water, and feel the loving warmth filling your being and travelling down along your arms, issuing as white-gold light from the palms of your hands. Form your symbol over the water and affirm that it is blessed.

Try not to touch your blessed water with your hands unless you are actually using it for blessing. Transfer it to small dropper bottles. People (especially children) can be blessed by a little of the water placed on the forehead, above and between the eyes. Objects can be blessed similarly and places can be sprinkled with consecrated water. Renew your blessed water regularly and pour stale water on to the Earth.

healing ritual

To heal a person or pet, rub some eucalyptus oil into a green candle with a little blessed water, too. Light the candle, feel peaceful and centred, and gaze at the flame. Imagine that the one you are healing is totally well. Do not imagine them getting better and do not try to drive out disease and discomfort. Concentrate on the positive. Repeat three times, 'With this charm, to you from me, Totally healthy shall you be.'

You can repeat this day after day, letting the candle burn down. Each time you finish, snuff out the candle and ground yourself thoroughly.

A candle flame is a wonderful aid to concentration when performing a ritual.

seasonal blessings

Walking barefoot on the Earth can make you feel close to the immense power of nature.

One of the best ways to benefit from the blessings of the Earth is to attune to the seasons and be aware of their special bounty. Nature worship focuses on eight seasonal festivals, honouring the unique gifts of each time of year. This is both sensuous and sacred, enabling you to be aware of bodily joy as well as spiritual meaning. It is a lovely way to feel connected to the Earth and 'held' by the Earth Mother.

On or around each of the festivals, go for a walk and note the feel of the air, the look of the countryside and all the impressions you get. Start a notebook or scrap-book dedicated to the seasons and discover what they mean to you. Collect mementoes, write a poem, paint a picture, make a cake or special dish. Soon you will feel a growing kinship with the Earth and a sense of richness and belonging that will empower you and all you do. This will increase year by year.

eight seasonal festivals

yule
This takes place on 22 December (22 June in the Southern Hemisphere). It is also the turn of the solstice and signifies rebirth, joy, gift-giving and family get-togethers. Burn red and green candles, pine and frankincense. Hang a symbol of your dearest wish on your tree (chocolate money for riches or an angel for a new baby) to come true in the coming year.

candlemas
Celebrated on 2 February (31 July in the Southern Hemisphere), this is a time of purity and creativity. Do something creative, make a resolution, make plans for projects with friends. Burn white candles, lavender and lemon. Take a candle round your house and bless each room with light.

spring equinox
Occurring on 21 March (22 September in the Southern Hemisphere), spring equinox is a time of hatching, budding. Clean the house, hold a tree-planting ceremony, burn candles of yellow and spring green, orange and sandalwood. Sprinkle blessed water on your garden.

May eve

Celebrated on 30 April (31 October in the Southern Hemisphere), this is a time of beauty, excitement, parties, dates and love-fests. Celebrate your body, invite friends for a feast. Burn candles of deep rose, ylang ylang and coriander. Massage your body by candlelight asking for the blessing of the Love Goddess.

midsummer

This takes place on 22 June (22 December in the Southern Hemisphere), and is a time of fulfilment, sweetness, barbecues, flower festivals and pilgrimage to special places or stone circles. Burn candles of vibrant floral colours, rose and geranium. Walk barefoot on the Earth or lie naked if that is possible.

Your body is a gift. Show that you honour it with a special massage on May eve.

loaf mass

This date, 31 July (2 February in the Southern Hemisphere), marks the harvest, achievement, harvest festivals, barn dances, visits to fields of corn and crop circles. Burn candles of gold and red, frankincense and clove. Bind three ears of wheat in red thread for health, wealth and wisdom, to hang on your hearth.

autumn equinox

Celebrated on 21 September (21 March in the Southern Hemisphere), autumn equinox is a time of dreaming, preserving, harvest suppers, meditation and study groups. Go berry-picking. Burn purple candles, cypress and lemon balm. Place amethyst beneath your pillow and note your dreams.

hallowe'en

This takes place on 31 October (30 April in the Southern Hemisphere) and is a time of mystery, knowledge, Hallowe'en parties, ghost hunts, murder-mystery, bonfire parties and story-telling. Visit barrow mounds in the mist. Burn black candles, patchouli and myrrh. Write what must go from your life on a paper and burn it.

The phases of the Moon can be celebrated by burning a candle. A black candle is suitable for dark moons.

Moon magic

As Queen of the Night, the Moon presides over our instincts and her rhythms affect our lives. To understand the effect the Moon has on you it is best to keep a lunar diary. Many people believe their energies grow when the Moon is waxing, reaching a peak at full Moon and generally reducing towards the quiet time of new Moon.

The Moon takes 29 days to move through a complete cycle. You will find the phase of the Moon published in most newspapers. Start to mark each new Moon and full Moon by lighting a candle on the day, as a recognition of the turning point. A white candle is best for a full Moon and a silver one for a new Moon. You might like to celebrate full Moon by having a glass of wine, a special meal or some other treat, and enjoying taking part in the cycle.

tasks to suit the Moon's phases

Certain psychic exercises lend themselves to specific phases of the Moon: when the Moon is waning is the time to do anything concerned with cutting down, reducing and shrinking. On page 93 we looked at how to cut the ties with someone with whom you have had a relationship. However, there may be other ties of a less specific nature or influences from which you might wish to be free.

Choose a day about a week before new Moon, cast your magic circle and light a black candle. Make sure you have a knife within your magic circle. Concentrate on 'blowing out' your auric sheath, like a balloon, as explained on page 66. When you have blown it out to about half a metre (1½ feet), visualize the negative influences as black tentacles attaching to your aura and slice them off with the knife. Do this each day until new Moon, letting the candle burn down a little bit more each day, until, on the day before new Moon you let it burn down to nothing. Now you are free to welcome the blessing of a fresh cycle.

charging up

Full Moon is a wonderful time to 'charge up' a lucky talisman. Obtain a piece of clear quartz that appeals to you. Cast your magic circle in the light of the Moon, if possible, and/or light a large white candle. If you can, obtain a calamus joss stick or burn powdered calamus as incense, because this herb is linked to the Moon and also with luck and protection.

Sitting in the light of the Moon (or candlelight) hold your quartz between your palms and think of all the times you have felt joyful and happy. Know that there are many, many more times like this ahead of you, more enjoyable, ecstatic times. Feel excited, uplifted and blessed. Let your feelings flow into the crystal and imagine it being 'charged up' with all these pleasurable and good sensations. When you have finished, ground yourself thoroughly. Place your crystal in a velvet pouch and carry it with you whenever you need some extra blessing. Your talisman can be cleansed and recharged from time to time.

You can charge up a piece of clear quartz to function as a lucky talisman.

ADVANCED MATTERS

So far we have looked at how to protect ourselves from subtle threats that are, however nasty they may seem, mostly accidental. Much more serious (but also less common) is psychic attack, though some occultists believe it is more frequent than we realize. Psychic attack is usually launched by someone who knows what to do with subtle energies, but very occasionally someone who is deeply malevolent and/or obsessed, or who is instinctively attuned in such matters, may succeed in doing this. There is also the possibility of having to deal with some non-human agency, such as a troublesome haunting.

In all of these situations, the 'psychic hygiene' you have been practising will stand you in good stead. On many occasions I have used a protective magic circle to keep some less-than-pleasant entity at bay, and if you are used to creating your 'bubble' you will be able to do this easily and swiftly. If your intuition is sufficiently honed, you will be able to spot anyone dodgy and keep away from them as much as possible. The same goes for places that feel sinister.

It is definitely best to keep away from playing with things like the 'Ouija' board, which seems to open an uncontrolled portal to the spirit realms and can lead to lots of trouble. Finally, if you encounter something that you feel is beyond your power to deal with, seek help from a contact in the Resources section on page 128.

Wiccans see the forces of light and darkness, of good and evil, as complementary.

the problem of evil

Some years ago I was asked to take part in a late-night phone-in radio chat-show about witchcraft and psychic matters. As my companions were a vicar and a professional sceptic, I was braced for a hard time, but nothing prepared me for the first caller, who brayed at me down the phone in a harsh, hysterical voice, 'All witches are evil – totally evil!'

I was tongue-tied, not just by the unfairness of the attack, but by its sheer ignorance. This woman had never met me and knew nothing of my beliefs, and yet she had such a dogmatic, unthinking concept of 'evil' that she was prepared to fling that at me. It was a chilling reminder of what it must have been like to live under threat of the Inquisition!

what is 'evil'?

So why did the caller think I was 'evil'? She wasn't very coherent on the subject, referring agitatedly to the Bible, with which she did not seem too familiar. She was probably an unhappy, repressed, anxious person who found it easier to see 'evil' around her than to look inwards at her own imperfections. We all suffer from this to some extent – we 'project' notions of evil on to others thus making the entire concept of evil problematic. What is subjective and what is not?

We are all capable of 'projecting' our Shadow on to others. This means that something we may hate about ourselves is more comfortably dealt with by hating this attribute or flaw in someone else. This projection presents problems in many human interactions, but it can be particularly difficult with regard to evil. Dogmatic religious sects may label anyone who does not agree with them as 'evil'. Whole races have been branded as 'evil' because they symbolize something that another race finds unacceptable. Those who shout loudest about evil provide a ready channel for it, by condemning, persecuting and destroying those they demonize, in the name of their beliefs. Clearly, we have to be very wary about branding anything or anyone as evil.

two sides of a single coin

Wiccans see the forces of light and darkness as complementary since without destruction there can be no creation. Evil is most probably a product of humanity, but that does not alter the fact that it is a real force, and often it feels like an entity. Evil is rather like love – very hard to define and describe, and yet we all know the feeling.

If you come across something or someone that you truly feel is evil, simply keep away. An evil person should be avoided and evil places should be shunned. Whatever the case, your best policy is one of non-engagement. Do not try to 'fight' the evil, whatever form it takes, unless you are very experienced and know what you are doing. Ask for protection and help from your spirit guides or guardian angels, letting them do any work that needs to be done, then fill your life and mind with the positive and life-affirming.

Life-affirming rituals with the right companions may work well in dispelling evil.

psychic attack

Very occasionally it is possible to come under deliberate psychic attack due to the envy, resentment or malice of another person. If you are unfortunate enough to be on the receiving end of this, then you may feel all sorts of unpleasant sensations, including panic attacks, inexplicable malaise, bad moods, lack of energy, a string of minor ailments and accidents and insomnia.

night terrors

Most characteristic of psychic attack is a specific kind of nightmare, in which the dreamer feels he or she is awake (which may be the case). The experience begins with a sensation of dread and the victim feels unable to

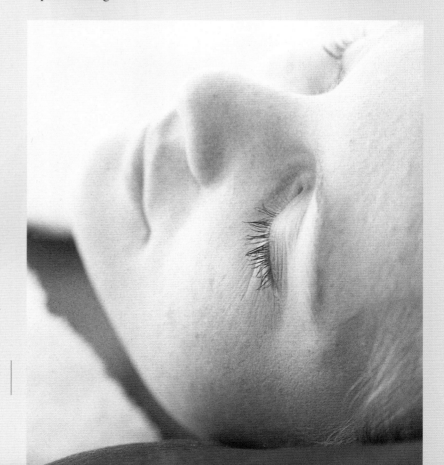

Psychic attack can result in disturbed sleep and a specific kind of nightmare.

move, while becoming aware of someone or something in the room – this 'entity' may be sensed or seen as a dark shape. The entity approaches the sleeper and usually moves on top of him or her. The victim feels that there is a great weight on his or her chest, may be unable to move and may hear voices or other sounds. Needless to say, a feeling of terror and powerlessness results from this contact.

The episode ends when the attacking entity detaches itself and disappears. Totally exhausted, the victim tends to fall into a deeper sleep, waking in the morning feeling tired and drained. Such an attack may come from a psychic vampire who draws on the etheric energy of another; whether the 'attack' is intended to cause harm or to leach energy, the effect is equally unpleasant and damaging.

playing on your weaknesses

Perhaps the scariest thing about psychic attack is that it is 'programmed' to find your weak spots, even if the attacker does not know what they are. We are all capable of neuroses and irrational fears, and even the most strong-minded may find it hard to cope with life if they are being besieged by malevolence.

How are such attacks achieved? It is possible to use rituals and exercises in order to send negative thoughts and create harm. It is also possible that a person can do this subconsciously, and while they may be aware of a desire to harm, they may not realize that they are being successful in projecting their wishes. In the same way that some people have a knack for doing good and creating love and warmth, others have a 'talent' for the opposite. Psychic attack can be harder to deal with if it comes from an ex-partner or from a family member. In this instance, it may be best to enlist the help of a friend who understand such matters, so that someone may take care of the physical and practical side, while someone else operates on the subtle planes.

While such attacks might understandably be described as 'evil', and may involve much that is truly evil, it is not as simple as that – you can't walk away from this as you might from an evil building or individual. Such evil is abstract and demonic – psychic attack is practical and all too human. It has to be dealt with on that basis.

dealing with psychic attack

Sharing your anxieties with someone who understands will strengthen and support you.

The majority of attackers cannot resist trying to find out if their attack has been successful; your attacker will be drawn to you, as the murderer to the scene of the crime. Even if the perpetrator is acting largely unconsciously, his or her obsession with you is bound to reveal itself.

If you really are under attack, then it is time to take the gloves off. More is needed than maintaining harmony and balance, and while you certainly do not wish to be drawn into sending malevolence yourself, it is necessary to send the harm firmly back from whence it came. Think of this in terms of martial arts: where the person under attack uses the weight and force of the attacker to unsettle and overthrow the aggressor.

When under attack you will soon learn who is the cause; let them have their nastiness back, where it belongs. Here are some hints:

- Go through the exercises in this book systematically and repeatedly – cleansing, strengthening and protecting. Do not meditate or open your chakras, unless you are quite sure you are in a protected state (which is unlikely if you are under attack).

- Adapt the 'Breaking the ties that bind' ritual (see page 93) to deal with the person attacking you, leaving out the rose petals and changing the last line to 'Apart and safe' instead of 'Apart and happy'.

- Avoid discussing the matter with anyone apart from your closest and most trusted friends who understand and accept the concept of psychic attack. There is no need to let your attacker know you are engaging with them. Wiccans have a saying: 'Know, will, dare – and be silent!'

- Another Wiccan saying goes: 'Where there's fear, there's power!' Now you may assume that the fear is yours and the power is someone else's – wrong! If you are afraid, turn your fear to anger and outrage.

- Seek help and support. Get true support of various kinds from magical friends who will help with enacting the rituals and therapists (to help with your own psychological aspects).

- Ask your guardian spirits to act for you or send your power animal. However, if you have not done the meditations to contact these entities, now is not the time to do so.

- Laugh as much as you can!

- Do not 'go into' your fears, trying to rationalize, analyze and overcome them – all you will do is to feed the fear. Walk away, actually or metaphorically.

- Strange as it may seem, sensitive people often feel sympathy for their attacker and guilt at retaliating, especially if the person has been a partner or friend, but these are feelings you cannot indulge if you are to remain intact, so switch into detachment and rationality. You deserve to survive, so fight!

- Tackle any practical matters involving property and money, home security and that sort of thing efficiently and firmly.

Simple laughter is a wonderful antidote to evil – remember the Boggart in the Harry Potter books?

self-protection

While it is advisable to seek the help of someone more experienced with these sorts of attacks, there are exercises you can do to defend yourself. Keep in your mind and in your heart the knowledge that you are not helpless.

melt your fear

1 Chose an attractive glass bowl and fill it with luke-warm water. Colour the water with your favourite food colour, if you wish. You will also need some ice-cubes.

2 Sweep out your space and create a protective magic circle. Burn a frankincense joss stick. Name an ice-cube for each of your fears.

3 Drop the ice-cubes into the warm water and watch them dissolve. Affirm that your fears have dissolved.

4 Dismantle your magic circle, pour the water on to the Earth and give thanks. This exercise is best performed with a waning Moon.

reflect back the harm

1 You need a mirror and a sunny day. First cleanse your mirror with spring water and pat it dry with a clean white cloth.

2 Lift your mirror up to reflect the Sun. Hold it for a few moments, then circle clockwise, saying, 'South, west, north, east, far and wide. Fear, hatred, harm, pain, cast aside.' (In the Southern Hemisphere circle anti-clockwise and change the rhyme to 'South, east, north, west ...').

3 Circle round faster and faster until you feel the power rise to a crescendo. Send the power into the mirror and place your now charged-up mirror to reflect harm back at the sender, at the window, desk or door.

4 Periodically cleanse and recharge your mirrors, preferably at the full Moon.

spirits in a bottle

1 This is a powerful ritual; plan it for three days before the new Moon.

2 Place nine rusty iron nails in an old wine bottle and say: 'I name you for pain'.

3 Add some vinegar and say, 'I name you for bitterness.' Follow this with some curdled milk, saying, 'I name you for fear.'

4 Place a cork on the bottle and shake it, saying, 'Evil bottled truly, tightly, I send you where you belong rightly.' Shake it, putting all your anger into the movement. (Note: Be very careful not to loosen the cork!)

5 Take the bottle outside, dig a hole in the earth away from any precious plants or waterways. Say: 'Earth ancient, wise, now take this brew, Let it flow right, I trust to you.'

6 Empty the bottle into the hole, shaking out all the contents. Cover the hole carefully. Cleanse the bottle with warm water, followed by spring water with salt. Leave it in sunshine and place in it an aquamarine tumble-stone.

crystal arrows

1 Obtain four small black obsidian wands or four tumble-stones. If the latter, you will also need four pieces of black paper, cut into arrowhead shapes.

2 Place the arrows or wands, with the stones on top of them, pointing to each of the cardinal directions around a white candle. Light the candle and affirm that the arrows are sending out aggressive energies to repel harm. Do this as often as you feel necessary. See the illustration on page 23.

index

acknowledgements and resources

Resources

The Spiritualist Association of Great Britain, 33 Belgrave Square, London, SW1X 8QB

Spiritualists' National Union, Redwoods, Stansted Hall, Stansted, Essex, CM24 8UD

Institute of Spiritualist Mediums, 20 Oakhurst Avenue, East Barnet, Hertfordshire, EN4 8DL

The College of Psychic Studies, 16 Queensberry Place, London, SW7 2EB

The Pagan Federation, PO Box 7097, London, WC1N 3XX

The British Society of Dowsers, Sycamore Barn, Hastingleigh, Ashford, Kent, TN25 5HW

National Federation of Spiritual Healers, Old Manor Farm Studio, Church Street, Sunbury-on-Thames, Middlesex, TW16 6RG

Picture credits

Special photography: Octopus Publishing Group Ltd/Russell Sadur
Other photography: AA Photolibrary/Britt Erlanson 121. **Alamy**/acestock 88. **Corbis** 24, 45; /Bettmann 19; /Cameron 12; /Edward S. Curtis 106; /Craig Tuttle 46; /Roger Wood 78; /Larry Williams/zefa 42; /Karen Zukowski/zefa 110. **Getty Images** 71 bottom, 73; /Alistair Berg 34; /Sandro Boticelli 80; /MECKY 103; /Martine Mouchy 66. **Imagesource** 52, 58 top. **Octopus Publishing Group Ltd** 14, 15, 71 top, 71 centre, 84 picture 4, 84 picture 3, 84 picture 2, 84 picture 1, 86, 116; /Fraser Cunningham 25; /Mike Hemsley/Walter Gardiner Photographers 112; /Ruth Jenkinson 61, 84 bottom; /Adrian Pope 95; /Russell Sadur 4, 7, 56, 57, 90, 117; /David Sarton 44; /Ian Wallace 58 bottom, 118. **PhotoDisc** 9, 20, 40, 70. **Photolibrary Group** 35. **Science Photo Library**/Geoff Kidd 94.

Executive Editor Sandra Rigby
Editor Camilla Davis
Executive Art Editor Sally Bond
Designer Rebecca Johns, Annika Skoog for Cobalt I D
Photographer Russell Sadur
Picture Research Taura Riley
Production controller Audrey Walter